HOTSP...
COS...
COSTA D...

Written by Teresa Fisher, updated by Jane Egginton
Front cover photography courtesy of Thomas Cook Tour Operations Ltd

Original concept by Studio 183 Limited
Series design by Bridgewater Books
Cover design/artwork by Lee Biggadike, Studio 183 Limited

Produced by the Bridgewater Book Company
The Old Candlemakers, West Street, Lewes, East Sussex BN7 2NZ, United Kingdom
www.bridgewaterbooks.co.uk
Project Editor: Emily Casey Bailey
Project Designer: Lisa McCormick

Published by Thomas Cook Publishing
A division of Thomas Cook Tour Operations Limited
PO Box 227, Units 15-16, Coningsby Road, Peterborough PE3 8SB, United Kingdom
email: books@thomascook.com
www.thomascookpublishing.com
+ 44 (0) 1733 416477

ISBN-13: 978-1-84157-522-3
ISBN-10: 1-84157-522-4

First edition © 2006 Thomas Cook Publishing
Text © 2006 Thomas Cook Publishing
Maps © 2006 Thomas Cook Publishing
Head of Thomas Cook Publishing: Chris Young
Project Editor: Diane Ashmore
Production/DTP Editor: Steven Collins

Printed and bound in Spain by Graficas Cems, Navarra, Spain

All rights reserved. No part of this publication may be reproduced, stored in a retrieval system or transmitted, in any form or by any means, electronic, mechanical, recording or otherwise, in any part of the world, without prior permission of the publisher. Requests for permission should be made to the publisher at the above address.

Although every care has been taken in compiling this publication, and the contents are believed to be correct at the time of printing, Thomas Cook Tour Operations Limited cannot accept any responsibility for errors or omission, however caused, or for changes in details given in the guidebook, or for the consequences of any reliance on the information provided. Descriptions and assessments are based on the author's views and experiences when writing and do not necessarily represent those of Thomas Cook Tour Operations Limited.

CONTENTS

SYMBOLS KEY 4

INTRODUCTION 5

Map of Costa del Sol &
   Costa de Almería......................6

Getting to know the Costa
   del Sol & Costa de Almería......8

The best of the Costa del
   Sol & Costa de Almería............9

RESORTS 11

Estepona 12

San Pedro de Alcántara 16

Puerto Banús.................................20

Marbella 24

Fuengirola.....................................30

Benalmádena Costa......................36

Torremolinos.................................42

Nerja..46

Almerimar.....................................50

Roquetas..52

Aguadulce.....................................54

EXCURSIONS 55

Sevilla 56

Gibraltar (UK)...............................62

Ronda..66

White towns 70

Mijas..72

Córdoba...76

Málaga 80

Granada 84

Mojácar 88

Almería..92

LIFESTYLES 95

Food & drink 96

Menu decoder 100

Shopping 102

Kids 104

Sports & activities 106

Festivals & events 108

PRACTICAL INFORMATION 111

Preparing to go 112

During your stay 116

INDEX 125

ACKNOWLEDGEMENTS 128

HOTSPOTS

SYMBOLS KEY
The following is a key to the symbols used throughout this book:

- **i** information office
- **🚌** bus stop
- **✉** post office
- **✝** church
- **🚆** train station
- **🛡** police station
- **✈** airport
- **↘** tip
- **🛍** shopping
- **🍴** restaurant
- **☕** café
- **🍸** bar
- **◉** fine dining

---

t telephone **f** fax **e** email **w** website address
a address **○** opening times **❶** important
€ budget price **€€** mid-range price **€€€** most expensive
★ specialist interest ★★ see if passing ★★★ top attraction

INTRODUCTION
Getting to know the Costa del Sol and the Costa de Almería

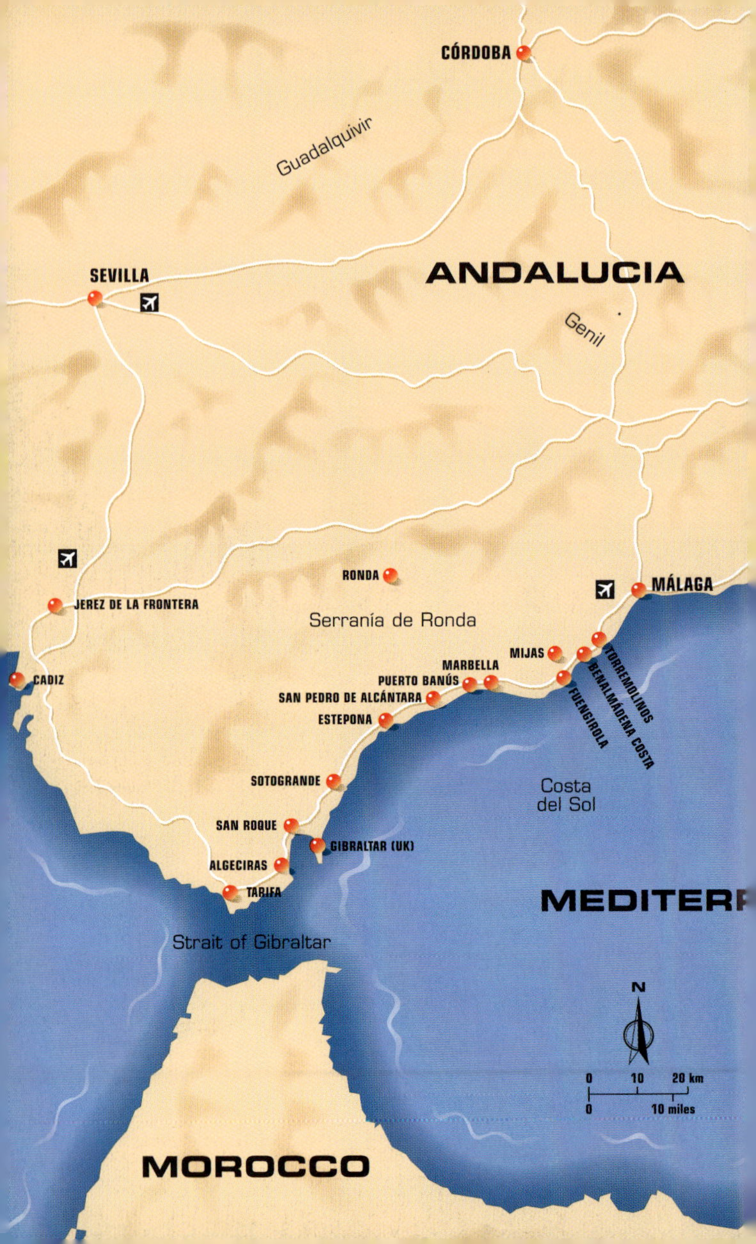
CÓRDOBA
Guadalquivir
SEVILLA
ANDALUCIA
Genil
RONDA
MÁLAGA
JEREZ DE LA FRONTERA
Serranía de Ronda
MIJAS
TORREMOLINOS
BENALMÁDENA COSTA
FUENGIROLA
MARBELLA
PUERTO BANÚS
SAN PEDRO DE ALCÁNTARA
CADIZ
ESTEPONA
SOTOGRANDE
Costa del Sol
SAN ROQUE
GIBRALTAR (UK)
ALGECIRAS
TARIFA
MEDITERR
Strait of Gibraltar
N
0
10
20 km
0
10 miles
MOROCCO

Costa de Almería

JAÉN

GRANADA
Sierra Nevada
3482 m
Las Alpujarras

COMPETA

NERJA

MOTRIL

ALMERIMAR

ROQUETAS

AGUADULCE

ALMERÍA

MOJÁCAR

MEAN SEA

Inset map

Bay of Biscay
Atlantic Ocean
FRANCE
PORTUGAL
ANDORRA
COSTA DEL SOL
Mediterranean Sea
COSTA DE ALMERÍA
MOROCCO
ALGERIA

INTRODUCTION

Getting to know the Costa del Sol and Costa de Almería

The 'Sun Coast' of the Costa del Sol and Costa de Almería, which stretches along the Mediterranean from Gibraltar in the west to Mojácar in the east, is one of the most popular tourist destinations in Europe. Certainly, it is one of Europe's best-equipped holiday playgrounds. Such highly-developed resorts as Torremolinos, Benalmádena, Fuengirola and Marbella cater for every taste and pocket, combining the attractions of sandy beaches, top-notch sporting facilities, lively bars and restaurants, an exhilarating nightlife and an exceptional climate.

East of Nerja, the Costa de Almería stretches round to Mojácar. Less busy and built up than the Costa del Sol, this section of the coast is largely devoted to horticulture, producing vast quantities of intensively grown salad crops and exotic fruits. Its small resorts appeal mainly to those seeking the more quiet beaches.

● *Andalucía offers visitors stunning scenery*

INTRODUCTION

ANDALUCÍA

On a typical day, you might get up late and spend your time sunbathing, swimming, eating and drinking, with a lazy siesta to occupy the greater part of the afternoon. But what if you get tired of lying on the beach all day? Then, take time to explore the rest of the famous and fascinating Andalucía region – the land of bullfighting, flamenco and sherry. Over the years, various invaders have left their mark on the countryside, including the Moors, who ruled the region for seven centuries and named it al-Andalus. The enchanting pueblos blancos (white towns) dotted about the countryside date from this period, as do many of the treasures of the principal cities, Córdoba and Granada, and Sevilla, the vibrant capital of Andalucía.

This region of sleepy whitewashed villages, historical cities and stunning landscapes (ranging from some of the highest mountains in Spain to seemingly endless sandy beaches) is also the spirited and vibrant land of country fiestas, electrifying nightlife, flamenco shows and distinctive cuisine. The variety and spirit of Andalucía, combined with all the fun of a beach-resort holiday, is what draws millions of visitors from all over the world to make southern Spain Europe's number-one holiday destination.

The best of the Costa del Sol and Costa de Almería

MUST-SEE SIGHTS

- **Almería's Alcazaba** (page 92) One of Spain's most impressive Moorish castles.
- **Las Alpujarras** (page 92) A wonderful area for hill walking or mountain biking, famed for its *jamón serrano*.
- **The Caves of Nerja** (page 46) With their spectacular rock formations and prehistoric paintings.
- **Córdoba** (page 76) Especially La Mezquita (the Great Mosque), one of the finest Moorish buildings in the world.

INTRODUCTION

- **Granada** (page 84) Home of the Alhambra Palace – known as the eighth wonder of the world – and its refreshing Generalife Gardens.
- **Marbella's Casco Antiguo, or Old Town** (page 25) With its picturesque main square, the Plaza de los Naranjos.
- **Mojácar** (page 88) Idyllic *pueblo blanco* – a hilltop village with a gorgeous beach nearby.
- **Puerto Banús** (page 20) Andalucía's most sophisticated marina with its luxury yachts, trendy shops, restaurants and bars.
- **The Rock of Gibraltar** (page 63) With its staggering views across the Straits to Africa.
- **Ronda** (page 66) With its famous bullring, ancient bridge and amazing setting high above the Guadalevín river.
- **Sevilla** (page 56) The capital of Andalucía – full of atmosphere and numerous historic buildings, including the largest Gothic cathedral in the world.
- **White towns** (page 70) The charming *pueblos blancos* of inland Andalucía, around Ronda and Nerja.

BEST ACTIVITIES

- Barter for local produce and handicrafts at **Fuengirola's Tuesday market** – the biggest and best market on the coast.
- Join a **boat excursion** to explore the coastline and to visit neighbouring resorts, or go on a dolphin safari.
- Pass the hours away lingering over a drink and **celebrity-spotting** beside the ostentatious gin palaces of glamorous Puerto Banús.
- Ride a **burro-taxi** (donkey-taxi) through the narrow streets of Mijas. Especially good fun for children.
- Eat the freshest of **fish** from one of La Carihuela's *chiringuitos* (beach restaurants) in Torremolinos.
- Taste the local sweet **wines** of Málaga and Frigiliana. Be warned, they are extremely potent.
- See a flamenco show in Sevilla.
- Try some of the **local cuisine** – tapas bars are a good starting point for tasting regional dishes.

RESORTS
Places under the sun

CALLE PORTADA
C ANTERO
CALLE CARIDAD
CALLE MALAGA
CALLE REAL
AVENIDA DE ESPAÑA
CHIRINGUITO
C MADRID
CALLE CADIZ
C SAN MIGUEL
CALLE ZARAGOZA
C EXTREMADURA
C LOZANO
C SAN JOSE
C SAN CAYETANO
AV VALENCIA
Playa de la Rada
CALLE PORTADA
PLAZA MANILVA
PLAZA ANTONIA GUERRERO
CALLE SAN ANTONIO
CALLE REYES
C CONCEPCION
CALLE HUERTO
CALLE PINTADO
CALLE TERRAZA
C A SUAREZ DE FIGUEROA
CALLE REAL
CHIRINGUITO
CASSA DE LA CULTURA
PZ DE LOS MISIONEROS
PLAZA DE LAS FLORES
PLAZA SAN FRANCISCO
C SIRENA
C MANZANARES
MEDITERRANEAN SEA
PLAZA DEL RELOJ
CALLE VILLA
C RAPHAEL
CHIRINGUITO
AYUNTAMIENTO
PLAZA AUGUSTO SAUREZ
PLZA CAÑADA
C POZO DE LOS PALOS
CALLE SEVILLA
C TORREJON
C CRUZ
C MONDEJAR
CALLE GENALGUACIL
CALLE REAL
AVENIDA DE ESPAÑA
PASEO MARITIMO PEDRO MANRIQUE
Playa de la Rada
C JUBRIQUE
PLAZA POZO PRADO
C CARAVACA
C NUEVA
PUERTO PESQUERO
C AFRICA
N
0
200 m
0
200 yds
MARINA
PLAYA DEL CHRISTO
CHIRINGUITO

Estepona
up-and-coming fishing town

The beachfront resort of Estepona has an air of upward mobility about it, and is quietly becoming one of the most fashionable places on the western Costas. Its pleasure marina is making glamorous Puerto Banús look to its laurels, while its golf courses attract many well-known international faces. Estepona, though, caters better for young families than the jet set. It makes no sightseeing demands on visitors, but there are few more relaxing places for a stroll than its tidy, palm-lined esplanades. For a drink and a good meal, head for the pavement cafés and restaurants around the jasmine-scented Plaza de las Flores, its aptly named flower-filled main square.

This modest, low-rise town spreads along a large expanse of beach. Its economic mainstays once revolved around fishing and citrus-growing – the streets in the old quarter all have charming ceramic name-plaques decorated with lemons. Unlike some parts of the Costas, agriculture and fishing have not entirely given way to the demands of tourism, and the town still has an unpretentious and refreshingly Spanish air. The quiet, flattish coastline is guarded by ancient fortresses, some dating from Roman or Phoenician times. Some distance inland, the road through the Serranía Bermeja climbs through forests where a unique species of fir tree called the *pinsapo* flourishes. From the Refugio de los Reales *mirador*, spectacular views extend as far as Gibraltar.

BEACHES
Estepona manages a 21 km (13 mile) stretch of coastline, and proudly waves a Blue Flag (the EU's quality stamp) on several of its beaches. The main strand is the long, sandy **Playa de la Rada**, punctuated by *chiringuitos* (beach bars) and the wooden watchtowers of the lifeguards. **Playa del Cristo**, near the marina, is a delightful oyster-shaped cove of sheltered, gently shelving sand, ideal for children. If you prefer life in the buff, head eastwards for the **Costa Natura**, Spain's oldest naturist resort.

RESORTS

THINGS TO SEE & DO

Golf ★★
Estepona has five local golf courses and several championship links around the smart *urbanización* of Sotogrande, which makes the region a paradise for dedicated golfers. The superb **Valderrama** course rose to fame when it hosted the Ryder Cup in 1997. ⓐ 11310 Sotogrande ⓣ 956 79 12 00 ⓦ www.valderrama.com

Polo ★
For a classy spectator sport with a difference, head for Sotogrande, near Estepona, where British and Argentinian teams practise their chukkas during the winter, on Spain's only permanent polo field. Tuition available. ⓐ Santa María Polo ⓣ 956 61 00 12/61 01 32

Selwo ★★★
A successful safari park with over 2000 exotic species, from giraffes to panthers, in their natural habitat. There are also daily shows. ⓐ Carretera N340, Km 162.5 ⓣ 902 19 04 82 ⓦ www.selwo.es ⓘ Admission charge.

RESTAURANTS (see map on page 12)

Bar Los Rosales €€ ❶ Serious fishy tapas in a quiet back street. ⓐ Calle Damas 12 ⓣ 952 79 29 45 ⓛ Closed Sat eve, Sun and 15 Nov–15 Dec

Casa de mi Abuela €€ ❷ Rustic decor and hearty Argentinian platters of chargrilled meat. ⓐ Calle Caridad 54 ⓣ 952 79 19 67 ⓛ Closed Tues and May

El Cenachero €€ ❸ A good bet. ⓐ Near Club Náutico. at the far end of the pleasure harbour ⓐ Puerto Deportivo ⓣ 952 80 14 42

La Gamba € ❹ Unpretentious seafood tapas bar, with fried fish and garlic chicken. ⓐ Calle Terraza 25 ⓣ 952 80 56 07 ⓛ Open Fri–Wed

ESTEPONA

Heladería Vitín € ⑤
Try ice creams such as an *horchata* or a *granizado* overlooking the square.
ⓐ Plaza de las Flores

Marisqueíra El Galiván del Mar €€€ ⑥
Great seafood restaurant in one of the old town's prettiest plazas. ⓐ Plaza Doctor Arce ⓣ 952 80 28 56 ⓞ Open Tues–Sun

Mesón Genaro €€ ⑦
Typical Iberian hams, snails and authentic tapas in a rustic setting. ⓐ Calle Rocío Jurado 15 ⓣ 952 80 44 38 ⓞ Open Thurs–Tues

Robbies €€€ ⑧
Popular English-run restaurant with snazzy decor. ⓐ Jubrique 11 ⓣ 952 80 21 21 ⓞ Dinner only 20.00–22.30 ⓞ Closed Mon, Feb and early Dec

▲ *Estepona's main square*

Get up early and see the fish market down by the Puerto Pesquero. Estepona has one of the Costa del Sol's largest fleets, and the harbour is a hive of activity as the night's catch is landed on the quaysides. It's mostly over by 07.00, just in time for breakfast.

RESORTS

San Pedro de Alcántara
a foothold in the past

West of Marbella, the little town of San Pedro nestles on a broad strip of fertile coastal lowland sheltered by rugged hills. It is less well known than its glitzy neighbours, but Costa del Sol experts recognize a good thing when they see it. Many expatriates have chosen to settle here, giving the place a more permanent, residential feel than some of the holiday resorts, and its stylish interior-design boutiques and smart little restaurants are well patronized. All around, large, elegant private villas lie masked behind walls and subtropical gardens – if you're sharp-eyed enough, you may spot some famous faces.

San Pedro dates from the 1860s, when it was established as a model farming community with an agricultural training school. Today many of its country estates are prosperous tourist enclaves or golf courses. Much of the town lies inland behind the coastal highway, and it's a fair step down to the beach. There's less nightlife here than in Marbella or Puerto Banús, but its plus points include a well-managed stretch of quiet, clean seafront and three of the most interesting archaeological remains anywhere on the coast. The neatly kept old town centres on the shady Avenida Marqués del Duero, lined with enticing shops and cafés, orange trees and fountains. Behind, on Plaza de la Iglesia, twin palm trees frame the white facade of San Pedro's charming parish church.

THINGS TO SEE & DO
Archaeological remains ★★
Behind the beach at Las Bovedas lies a Roman bath house with a wood-fired heating system, and a 4th-century basilica with a beautiful font. Four kilometres (2.5 miles) east at Río Verde is a Roman villa decorated with delightful mosaics showing kitchen utensils.
🕿 952 78 13 60 🕒 Free guided tours on Tues, Thurs and Sat at noon. Meet at the archway tourist office (see Tip box, page 19) on the Carretera N340, Km 170.5 (no transport provided, but you may be able to get a lift)

SAN PEDRO DE ALCÁNTARA

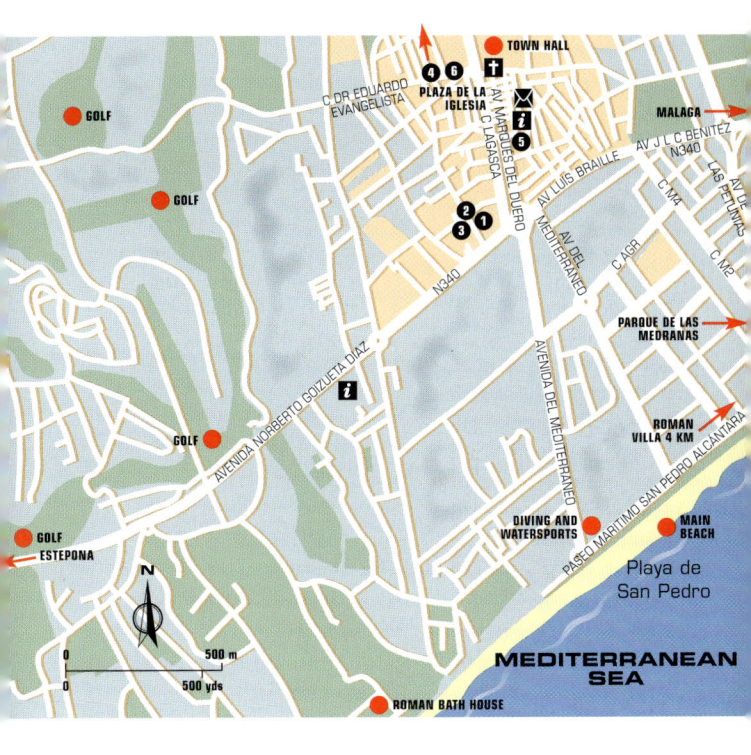

Bowling ★
Visitors are welcome at the tranquil bowling club, **Bolera San Pedro**.
ⓐ Calle Toledo ⓣ 952 78 32 41; call ahead to check availability

Cable-skiing ★★
Waterskiing with a difference; you're towed along a fixed overhead wire – easier than an erratic, fast-moving boat. Perfect your skills on a calm inland lake. **Cable Ski Marbella** ⓐ Parque de las Medranas ⓣ 952 78 55 79 ⓦ www.cableskimarbella.com ⓞ Open 11.00–15.00 and 16.00–21.00

RESORTS

SHOPPING

Street Market Every Thursday there's a lively market near the Sports Pavilion for those with an eye for a bargain.
Bookworld España For something to read, try this excellent English-language bookshop on the main street. ⓐ Residencia Fuentemar ⓣ 952 78 85 65 ⓞ Open Mon–Fri 10.00–14.00 and 17.00–20.00, Sat 10.00–14.00
Viva Stylish houseware store, with small, portable items suitable as presents (bottle-stoppers, glass and ceramic ornaments) ⓐ Calle Lagasca ⓣ 952 78 15 34 ⓞ Closed Sat eve and Sun
Vassiliki This is a popular backwater for local artists. For postcards, pottery, jewellery, ceramics and unique examples of local art, head for the shop called Katoi. ⓐ On the Ponti Road, next door to Mythos Taverna ⓣ 264 50 31 700

Riding ★★

Call a day ahead to book an hour's trek through the countryside with one of the instructors, at **San Pedro Riding School**. ⓐ Carril del Potril ⓣ 952 78 81 89 ⓞ Open Tues–Sun 09.30–20.30

BEACHES

There are fantastic water sports facilities at **Bora-Bora Beach**, including waterskiing, motorboats, canoes, rowboats, as well as scuba diving. ⓐ Urb. Lindavista, Calle Gitanilla

RESTAURANTS (see map on page 17)

Alfredo €€ ❶ Excellent game and fish tapas and grills in a lively atmosphere. ⓐ Calle Andalucía, Local 8 ⓣ 952 78 61 65

Andalucía € ❷ 'We offer the best value for money in the area', claims this popular restaurant. Fixed-price menus and local cooking. ⓐ Calle Andalucía, Local 4 ⓣ 952 78 22 93 ⓞ Open Sun–Fri

SAN PEDRO DE ALCÁNTARA

Caruso €€
3 Smart, modern restaurant serving popular dishes and adventurous daily specials. Calle Andalucía, Local 6 · 952 78 22 93 · Dinner only, Mon–Sat 19.30–23.30

El Gamonal €€
4 Some of the best cooking around, in a flower-filled, country setting off the Ronda road. Roast specialities. Camino La Quinta · 952 78 99 21 · Closed Wed and mid Jan–mid Feb

▲ *San Pedro's parish church*

Jardin del Vino €€
5 Sip a Pimms on a pavement table by the main street's shady gardens, or try the house sea bass in salt. Pasaje Las Palmeras 9 · 952 78 42 16 · Closed Sat (summer) and Wed (winter)

Mesón El Coto €€€
6 Lovely terrace restaurant high in the hills on the road to Ronda. Excellent cooking (seasonal game) and attentive service. Carretera de Ronda · 952 78 66 88 · Open 19.30–00.30

The unmissable giant arch over the coastal highway (N340) at San Pedro emblazoned with the sign MARBELLA contains a helpful regional tourist office (seaward side), which is open until midnight in summer.

RESORTS

Puerto Banús
pleasure port

Marbella's exclusive and world famous marina – Puerto Banús – just a short distance to the west, is the playground of the rich and famous, where the international jet set come to shop, socialize and party. It is the Costa del Sol's most celebrated port, filled with a dazzling collection of massive, ostentatious yachts and gin palaces operated by battalions of uniformed crew – very much the place to see and be seen. Behind the port, the 'Golden Mile' to Marbella throbs with nightspots and restaurants. Spot King Fahd's exotic Arabian palace, Mar Mar. Inland, the glitterati villas and exclusive country clubs of Nueva Andalucía stretch back into the hills.

This glamorous complex, named after its designer José Banús, was created in 1968, and its success has spawned a number of rival wannabes up and down the coast. Few, though, can boast the spectacular backdrop of rugged hills which gives the marina its photogenic setting. A village-like development of eye-catching, pantiled apartments in Spanish and Moorish styles surrounds the waterfront walkways, forming a seamless chain of eating places, bars and boutiques. As the sun sinks below the yardarm, beautiful people strut their stuff on the quaysides before leisurely making their way to the most fashionable nightlife venues.

THINGS TO SEE & DO
Golf ★★
No dedicated golfer should miss out on a visit to the **Marbella Golf and Country Club** (see page 25).

Aquarium Puerto Banús ★
A fascinating place for all the family, this aquarium is housed in an old watchtower. Displays include sharks, stingrays and octopuses. ❷ At the port ❶ 952 81 87 67

MARBELLA

MEDITERRANEAN SEA

Playa Puerto Banús

- PUERTO JOSÉ BANUS CLUB NAÚTICO
- CINES GRAN MARBELLA
- EL CORTE INGLÉS
- URBANIZACIÓN BENABOLA
- PORT
- AQUARIUM PUERTO BANÚS
- CASINO
- URBANIZACIÓN GRAY D'ALBION
- SAN PEDRO DE ALCÁNTARA
- URBANIZACIÓN ANDALACÍA MAR

Playa Nueva Andalacía

AVENIDA MALAGA
A. NACIONES UNIDAS
AVENIDA DE RIBERA
A JOSÉ BANUS
C. BENABOLA
AVENIDA PLAYAS DEL DUQUE
AVENIDA CADIZ

0 — 500 m
0 — 500 yds

RESORTS

RESTAURANTS (see map on page 21)

Azul Marino €€ ❶ Superb international fish cuisine served in a smart nautical decor in a magnificent prime waterfront location. ⓐ Muelle Ribera ⓣ 952 81 10 44 ⓛ Open noon–01.00 ⓦ www.buenas-mesas.com

La Caracola del Puerto €€ ❷ Try one of 16 different types of paella at this smart, waterfront fish restaurant. ⓐ Muelle Benabola 5 ⓣ 952 81 16 84 ⓛ Open Wed–Mon

Dalli's Pizza and Pasta Factory €€ ❸ Pizza and pasta combined in this cheap and cheerful Italian restaurant, with an adjoining café. ⓐ Avda Fontanilla ⓣ 952 81 86 23 ⓛ Open 19.00–01.00

Farggi's €€ ❹ A *salon de thé* with a mouth-watering selection of home-made ices and cakes. ⓐ Muelle Ribera

Finca Besaya €€€ ❺ This exclusive, relaxing hideaway is situated in an old avocado farm nestled high in the hills. Accomplished cooking. ⓐ Urb. Río Verde Alto ⓣ 952 86 13 86 ⓛ Open Tues–Sun 19.30–midnight ⓘ Booking essential; dress smartly

Red Pepper €€ ❻ Friendly Greek restaurant right on the quayside. ⓐ Muelle Ribera ⓣ 952 81 21 48 ⓛ Closed Sun

NIGHTLIFE

Casino ❼ Bring plenty of cash for an evening here! ⓐ Hotel Andalucía Plaza ⓣ 952 81 40 00 ⓛ Slot machines open from 16.00 hours; casino 20.00–05.00 ⓘ Dress smartly, and bring a passport

Cines Gran Marbella ❽ English-language films are shown in this seven-screen complex. ⓐ Paseo de la Ribera ⓣ 952 81 00 77 ⓦ www.cinesgranmarbella.com

PUERTO BANÚS

> **SHOPPING**
>
> 🛍️ **Boutique 007** Shop here for the latest in beach and club wear. ⓐ Muelle Ribera 4 ⓣ 952 81 13 95
> **El Corte Inglés** This massive department store and supermarket stocks just about everything! ⓐ Ramón Areces, Centro Comercial Costa Marbella, on the outskirts of Puerto Banús ⓣ 952 90 99 90 ⓛ Closed Sun (winter) ⓦ www.elcorteingles.es
> **Adolfo Dominguez** Spanish designer label at the slightly more affordable end of luxury fashion. ⓐ Ramón Areres ⓣ 952 90 60 20
> **Kosas** Embroidery specialists here will personalize a T-shirt for you while you wait. ⓐ Muelle Ribera J5
> **Market** A large flea market. ⓐ Held around the bullring of Nueva Andalucía. ⓛ Open Sat 09.00–14.00
> **Neck & Neck** Posh children's clothes in a street behind the waterfront. ⓐ Muelle Ribera 10A ⓣ 952 81 48 41

Comédia ⑨ One of the port's most popular and lively discos. ⓐ Plaza de la Comédia ⓛ Open midnight–05.00

Olivia Valére ⑩ Celebrated nightclub, and haunt of the rich and famous. Smart restaurant, sushi and piano bars. ⓐ Carretera Istán, Km 0.7, Nueva Andalucía ⓣ 952 82 88 61 ⓛ Restaurant open 21.00–01.00; nightclub open midnight–05.00

Sinatra Bar ⑪ Rub shoulders with the likes of Antonio Banderas in this laid-back, see-and-be-seen, waterfront bar. ⓐ Muelle Ribera 2

↘ Only a handful of authorized vehicles are allowed within the port area. Make for one of the underground car parks; preferably at the huge department store, El Corte Inglés. If you do any shopping there, you can park free of charge.

23

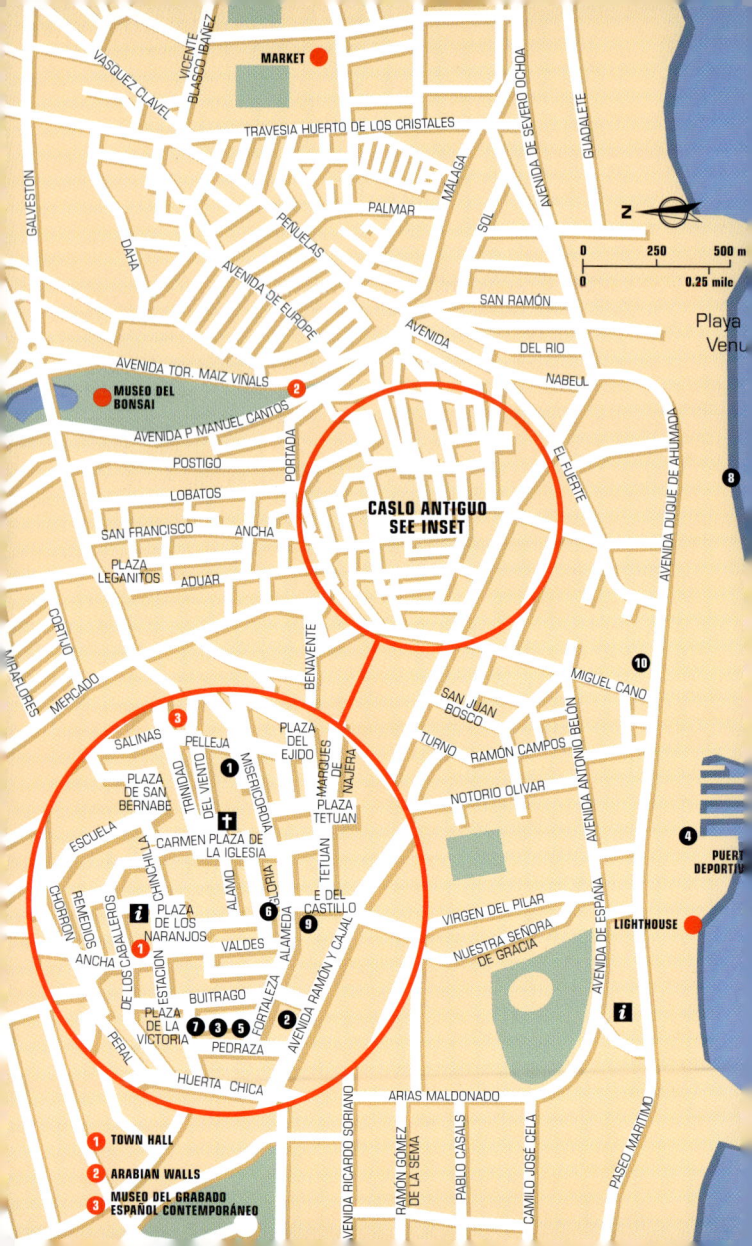

1. TOWN HALL
2. ARABIAN WALLS
3. MUSEO DEL GRABADO ESPAÑOL CONTEMPORÁNEO

MARBELLA

Marbella
party capital

Glamorous and cosmopolitan yet fiercely traditional at the same time, Marbella perfectly blends old with new and is considered by many to be the jewel of the resorts along the Costa del Sol.

The old town (*Casco Antiguo*) has been carefully and sympathetically maintained – a quaint pedestrian district of tiny squares and white-washed houses smothered in bougainvillea clusters round the postcard-pretty Plaza de los Naranjos, named after its orange trees. By contrast, modern Marbella centres around its designer-boutique-lined Avenida Ricardo de Soviano, and the seafront. In the evenings, its smart promenade becomes a catwalk for well-dressed Spanish families.

↘ Pick up a copy of the free English/Spanish listings booklet *Guía Marbella – Día y Noche* (*Leisure Guide – Day and Night*) from the tourist office (Plaza de los Naranjos) or your hotel reception, or check ⓦ www.andalucia.com/marbella

THINGS TO SEE & DO
Golf ★★
For anyone interested in golf there are many splendid courses in the area immediately around Marbella. So high is the standard of the golfing facilities that numerous top international players come here to practise during the winter, and some have permanent connections with the area. The swankiest clubs are situated mostly to the west in the hills of Nueva Andalucía. Most demand a handicap certificate, and require booking well in advance. Contact the tourist office for details.
Aloha Golf ⓐ Nueva Andalucía ⓦ www.clubdegolfaloha.com
Las Brisas ⓦ www.brisasgolf.com
La Quinta ⓦ www.laquintagolf.com
Marbella Golf and Country Club This exclusive course is on the Málaga side ⓐ Carretera N340, Km 188 ⓞ 952 83 05 00 ⓦ www.marbellagolf.com

RESORTS

Museo del Bonsai (Bonsai Museum) ★★
This unusual venture housed in a park near the old town has a fine collection of about 300 bonsai specimens attractively set amid water gardens. ⓐ Parque Arroyo de la Represa ⓣ 952 86 29 26 ⓞ Open 10.00–13.30, 16.30–20.00 (summer) and 10.00–13.30, 16.00–19.00 (winter) ⓘ Admission charge

Museo del Grabado Español Contemporáneo (Museum of Contemporary Spanish Engravings) ★
This important collection of engravings is on display in a fine old building (a former 17th-century hospital) near the Arab city walls. It provides a comprehensive overview of Spanish artistic trends since the 19th century, including works by Picasso, Miró and Dalí. ⓐ Calle Hospital Bazán ⓣ 952 82 50 35 ⓞ Open Tues–Sat 10.15–14.00, 17.30–20.30, and Sun 10.30–14.00 (summer); 10.00–14.00, 17.30–20.30 (winter), and Sun 10.30–14.00 ⓘ Admission charge

BEACHES & WATER SPORTS

The Marbella coastline has 26 km (16 miles) of attractive, well-tended sandy beaches. The central beaches stretch either side of the *puerto deportivo* (yacht marina) below elegant, traffic-free promenades. There are plenty of places to lounge beneath a parasol, showing off your latest designer swimwear. But many Marbella visitors seize the opportunity to enjoy energetic, high-tech water sports of all kinds. Magnificent facilities can be found at the beach clubs of the larger hotels, including excellent swimming pools.

Club Maritimo Scuba diving, sailing and windsurfing near Marbella's yacht harbour. ⓐ Puerto Deportivo ⓣ 952 77 25 04

Funny Beach Water-slides, bumper boats (an aquatic version of dodgems), mini-golf, jetskiing, go-karting, laser games and giant Scalextric. ⓐ Carretera N340, Km 184 ⓣ 952 82 33 59 ⓦ www.funnybeach.net

MARBELLA

Hotel Don Carlos Surfboard hire, pedalos and catamarans. 🅐 Carretera N340, Km 192 🕿 952 83 11 40 🌐 www.hoteldoncarlos.com

Hotel Gran Melia Don Pepe Motorboats, waterskiing, windsurfing, pedalos, and catamarans. 🅐 Jose Melia 🕿 952 77 03 00 🌐 www.donpepe-marbella.com

Hotel Marbella Club Motorboats, windsurfing, kitesurfing, waterskiing, pedalos, canoes and catamarans. 🅐 Blvd Principe Alfonso von Hohenlohe 🕿 952 82 22 11

Hotel Puente Romano Motorboats, windsurfing, kitesurfing, water-skiing, pedalos, canoes and catamarans. 🅐 Carretera N340, Km 177 🕿 606 48 80 68 (mobile) 🌐 www.puenteromano.com

EXCURSIONS
Mini cruise ★★
Travel by boat from Marbella to Puerto Banús. The journey takes approximately 30 minutes. 🅐 Victoria S, Marbella Marina 🕿 608 45 67 50 🕓 Departures from Marbella at regular intervals ℹ Dolphin-watching trips are also available

Ojén ★★
This picturesque mountain village lies about 10 km (6 miles) north of Marbella, high in the hills of the Sierra Blanca. Just beyond the village, in a forested game reserve, is the Refugio de Juanar, a charming hunting-lodge inn (🕿 952 88 10 00 🌐 www.juanar.com). This makes a good starting point for walks through the hills where you may catch sight of the rare Iberian ibex, a horned goat-like creature. If you don't feel energetic, just enjoy a good lunch. Ojén is on a bus route from Marbella. Jeep excursions, treks and mountain bike hire are organized by **Monte Aventura**. Ask your rep, hotel or the tourist office for more information. 🅐 Oficina de Turismo Rural, Plaza de Andalucía 1, Ojén 🕿 952 88 15 19 🌐 www.monteaventura.com

RESORTS

RESTAURANTS (see map on page 24)

Bar Altamirano € ❶ A place of genuine character, on a quiet square near the walls at the back of the old town. Tiled wall-plaques promise exotic sea fare: bleaks, saurels, elephant fish. ⓐ Plaza de Altamirano ❶ 952 82 49 32 ⓛ Open Thurs–Tues

Cafetería Marbella €€ ❷ A good bet for breakfast or coffee on Marbella's smartest shopping street near the shady Alameda Gardens. Plenty of terrace space. ⓐ Avenida Ramón y Cajal ❶ 952 86 11 44

El Estrecho € ❸ A real locals' tapas bar down a narrow alleyway. ⓐ Calle San Lázaro 12 ❶ 952 77 00 04 ⓛ Open Mon–Sat

Gulzar €€ ❹ A good-value Indian restaurant not far from the beach, with a plain but dignified interior. ⓐ Calle Camilo José Cela (near the Hotel Skol) ❶ 952 77 25 97 ⓛ Closed Mon (winter)

Marisquería La Pesquera €€ ❺ Highly rated seafood restaurant with shady tables on a pretty square. Try *dorado* (red mullet) or lobster. ⓐ Plaza de la Victoria ❶ 952 76 51 70 ⓦ www.lapesquera.com

Mena €€ ❻ The terrace restaurants on the main square are geared towards tourists, but this little place isn't bad value. Lovely setting in an old house with tables under the orange trees. ⓐ 10 Plaza de los Naranjos ❶ 952 77 15 97 ⓛ Open Mon–Sat noon–16.00 and 20.00–midnight

La Meridiana €€€ ❼ A special-occasion restaurant specializing in gourmet seafood dishes and to-die-for desserts. ⓐ Camino de la Cruz ❶ 952 77 61 90 ⓛ Dinner only ❶ Reservations essential

Palms € ❽ Beachside restaurant specializing in more interesting salads than most, as well as excellent catch-of-the-day fish dishes. ⓐ Playa de Venus

MARBELLA

SHOPPING

Marbella's smartest shopping street is **Ramón y Cajal**. The old town has lots of crafts and attractive souvenirs on sale. Marbella's street market takes place by the football stadium on Mondays.

Bravo One of Marbella's best leatherware shops – bags and shoes galore. ⓐ Ramón y Cajal 5 ⓣ 95 2773235

El Camino Traditional flamenco costumes and accessories for children and adults. ⓐ Calle Estación 2 ⓣ 95 2775004

Málaga Plaza Shopping complex with a range of boutiques on several floors and a café. ⓐ Armengual de la Mota 12 ⓣ 95 2614040

El Patio Andaluz € ❾ A simple but good value Spanish restaurant set in a pleasant, cool, flower-filled courtyard. ⓐ Calle San Juan de Dios 4

Santiago €€€ ❿ The suave but rather expensive seafront restaurant situated near the port has an excellent, and considerably less pricey tapas bar just round the corner. On offer is a splendid array of authentic Andaluz dishes served in a lively and very Spanish atmosphere. ⓐ Paseo Marítimo 5 ⓣ 952 77 00 78 ⓦ www.restaurantesantiago.com

NIGHTLIFE

Most of Marbella's liveliest nightlife centres on Puerto Banús (see page 22), or takes place in various hotels. Dress up, refuel your wallet and head for the cocktail bars of the **Marbella Club** or the **Puente Romano**. There are a few bars around Puerto Deportivo, but for some real action head to **Oh! Marbella** in Hotel Don Carlos, which has a popular disco that stays open to the small hours. ⓐ Carretera N340, Km 192 ⓣ 952 83 54 77

Playa de Los Boliches
Playa de Fuengirola
Playa de Santa Amalia
Playa del Castillo
MEDITERRANEAN SEA
MARKET
JEREZ
ROMERIA DEL ROCIO
JUAN SEBASTIAN ELCANO
JESUS SANTOS REIN
GÁLVEZ GUINACHERO
PARKILANDIA
CLUB NÁUTICO
PASEO MARITIMO REY DE ESPAÑA
AVDA ALCALDE CLEMENTE
MIGUEL BUENO
ISLA DE MENORCA
JOSE MORENO CARBONERO
MARTINEZ CATENA
MARKET
JACINTO BENAVENTE
MIJAS
CÓRDOBA
CASA DE LA CULTURA
SAN PANCRACIO
OVIEDO
CRUZ
JUAN GÓMEZ JUANITO
SAN RAFAEL
MARBELLA
CAMINO COIN
MARCONI
TRONCON
PALANGREROS
CUESTA
ZOO
CAMILO JOSÉ CELA
CAM JIEJO DE COIN
CAMINO DE SANTIAGO
PLAZA DE TOROS
MATEDERO
PARQUE ACUÁTICO DE MIJAS
AVDA CONDES DE SAN ISIDRO
MOLINO
CAMINO DE LA CONSESA
MÁLAGA
MIGUEL MARQUEZ
AVDA DE SANTA AMALIA
HÉROES DE BALER
AVDA MIRAMAR
RIO FUENGIROLA
N
0
1 km
0
0.25 mile
1
2
3
4
5
6
7
8
9
10
11
12
13
14
15
16
17
18
19
20
21
22

Fuengirola
cosmopolitan resort

Fuengirola is a lively and popular seaside resort with beautiful beaches, a vibrant nightlife and lots of attractions for all ages.

The beach is the centre of activity day and night. It is lined by one of the longest promenades on the Mediterranean (it takes about two hours to walk from one end to the other). Just behind the palm-lined walkway, the old fishermen's district of Santa Fé has retained its Andalucían character. Its narrow whitewashed streets contain some of the best restaurants in town, especially around the main square – Plaza de la Constitución – and along Calle Moncayo, nicknamed the 'Street of the Hungry'.

THINGS TO SEE & DO
Boat trips ★★
Daily fishing trips, dolphin-spotting and sunset cruises are all on offer at the marina.
Joren Maria II 952 44 48 81
The Dawn Approach 649 19 41 03 www.dawnapproach.co.uk

Fuengirola Zoo ★★
A simulated tropical rainforest and 75 species of animals are part of this revamped attraction. Avda Camilo Jose Cela 6 Open from 10.00

Parkilandia ★
Swings, slides, a trampoline, a bouncy castle, and mini-karting on the seafront. Puerto Deportivo, Pasejo Marítimo 952 58 12 86

Parque Acuático de Mijas ★★
Children love the water-slides, rapids, surf pools and other amusements at this refreshing water park, just ten minutes by shuttle bus from Fuengirola bus station. Carretera N340, Km 209 952 46 04 04 www.aquamijas.com Open Apr–Oct Admission charge

RESORTS

BEACHES

Fuengirola boasts one of the best seafronts of the entire Costa, with over 7 km (4.3 miles) of clean, sandy beaches, divided into restaurant-beach strips each renting out lounge chairs, parasols and pedalos. The central beaches of Santa Amalia, Castillo and Fuengirola lap the old town to either side of the port, while to the east the sand continues in an unending sweep past the hotel zones of Los Boliches and Torreblanca.

RESTAURANTS (see map on page 30)

Café Fresco €€ ❶ Excellent English-run restaurant with tasty soups, extensive salad bar, wraps, sandwiches and fresh, mixed juices like carrot, orange and ginger. ⓐ Las Rampas ⓣ 679 31 12 23

Cafetería Costa del Sol € ❷ The place to enjoy breakfast Spanish-style – *churros* dipped into a cup of thick, sticky hot chocolate. A great cure for a hangover! ⓐ Calle Marbella 3 ⓣ 952 47 17 09

Casa Flores € ❸ Typical bar serving Spanish food and tapas. ⓐ Avenida Condes San Isidro (in front of the Ayuntamiento)

La Langosta €€€ ❹ Long-established restaurant specializing in lobster, as its name suggests. Mussels in saffron and steaks in sauces are other notable dishes. ⓐ Fco Cano, Los Boliches 1
ⓣ 952 47 50 49 ⓞ Open Mon–Sat 19.00–midnight

SHOPPING

Shopping in Fuengirola ranges from cheap souvenir shops to high-class boutiques. For the best bargains, visit the **Tuesday morning market** – the largest and most colourful market on the Costa del Sol. ⓐ Avenida Jesús Santos Rein ⓞ Open 10.00–15.00. Or try **Centro Comercial Parque Miramar**, a modern shopping centre. ⓐ Avenida de la Encarnacion

◐ *One of Fuengirola's market stalls, the most colourful market in Costa del Sol*

Monopol €€ ❺ Rustic decor and unusual specialities, plus 'surprise' menus – blind dates on plates! ⓐ Calle Palangreros 7 ⓘ 952 47 44 48 ⓒ Open dinner only, closed Sun and mid-July–mid-Aug

Moochers €€ ❻ The only restaurant in the town centre with a roof terrace. Steaks, seafood, crepes and vegetarian specials, often with a jazz accompaniment. ⓐ Calle de la Cruz 7 ⓘ 952 47 71 54 ⓒ Open 19.00–01.00 ⓘ Booking is recommended

Mumtaz €€ ❼ Fuengirola's top Indian restaurant. ⓐ Calle Jaen (opposite Hotel Angela) ⓘ 952 47 71 21 ⓒ Open for dinner only

O Mamma Mia € ❽ Popular, family-orientated Italian restaurant with quick, friendly service. Good value for money. ⓐ Calle de la Cruz 23 ⓘ 95 2473251

Old Swiss House €€ ❾ *Rösti* and fondue, but plenty else too in this pleasant restaurant. ⓐ Marina Nacional 28, one block behind the beach ⓘ 952 47 26 06 ⓒ Open 13.00–15.30 and 19.00–midnight; closed Tues

RESORTS

El Sultán €€ ❿ Moroccan specialities in a lavish, Alhambra-like setting. Belly dancing at weekends. ⓐ Héroes de Baler ❶ 952 46 20 78 ⓒ Open Sat, Sun and holidays 13.00-16.00, closed Mon

Taberna Los Hermanos Alba €€ ⓫ Fried fish dishes and home-made desserts in a spacious blue and white dining room with terrace tables and tubs of orange trees. Try anchovies with lemon or grilled snapper. ⓐ Héroes de Baler 4 ❶ 952 47 41 67

Tomate €€ ⓬ Cheerful decor (red!) and shady patio tables. Interesting menu including pork and hazelnuts, smoked lamb in honey or ragout of venison. ⓐ Troncón 19 ❶ 952 46 35 59 ⓒ Open Tues–Sun 19.00

NIGHTLIFE

Arenas ⓭ One of the trendiest discos in town, with a spectacular laser show. ⓐ Avenida Jacinto Benavente, corner of Paseo Maritimo, near Hotel Las Palmeras ❶ Admission charge

The Cotton Club ⓮ Chilled-out atmosphere, the pick of the bunch. Live music most Thursdays. ⓐ Avenida Condes San Isidro 9

Irish Times ⓯ A civilized Irish bar serving a good pint of Guinness (of course!), with occasional live music; attractive patio. ⓐ Avenida Condes San Isidro 26

Ku'Damm Berlin ⓰ A popular German-style restaurant/bar which has live music located down by the harbour. ⓐ Puerto Deportivo, Local 12 ❶ 952 47 28 64

Linekers ⓱ This UK sports bar and fun pub, belonging to Gary's brother Wayne, has cheap beer (happy hour 17.00–19.00), pool tables, English DJs, karaoke and theme nights. ⓐ Puerto Deportivo, Club Náutico ❶ 952 47 62 85 ⓦ www.linekars-bar.com

◬ *The main promenade in Fuengirola*

London Pub ⓲ Home from home – a real city pub. By day, the theme is sport, giving you the opportunity to watch live broadcasts of top events worldwide. By night, DJs play dance music, getting you in the mood for the Underground Disco next door. ⓐ Paseo Marítimo ⓣ 952 47 63 87 ⓦ www.thelondonpubspain.com ⓞ Open 10.00–04.00

Mai Tai ⓳ From 20.00 to midnight is 'Strictly Ballroom' (foxtrot, tango, salsa) then midnight to 07.00 is 'Strictly Clubbing' (soul, disco, rock and house). ⓐ Paseo Marítimo, near Hotel El Puerto ⓘ Admission charge

Ministry ⓴ A welcome break from the euro pop standard, this nightclub is a hit and often features top names from the international DJs circuit, though it has no connection with London's Ministry of Sound. ⓐ Paseo Marítimo ⓞ Open Wed–Sat 23.00–dawn (happy hour midnight–04.00) ⓘ Free entry except at weekends

Old Town Café ㉑ A small, traditional bar, very popular with young Spanish. ⓐ Paseo Marítimo ⓣ 952 58 07 39 ⓦ www.oldtown-cafe.com

Video Café ㉒ If clubbing is not your scene but you like to let your hair down, come here after 21.00 for a wild night of cocktails and karaoke. ⓐ Avenida Jacinto Benavente ⓣ 952 47 18 66 ⓞ Open Mon–Sat 10.00–02.00 (happy hour 20.00–22.00)

RESORTS

Benalmádena Costa
round-the-clock fun

Benalmádena Costa is a lively, purpose-built holiday resort with a wide variety of entertainment for all the family, good water sports facilities, shops, bars and restaurants appealing to all tastes and budgets. The stunning marina greatly enhances the resort's appeal, and its many bars and nightclubs have made Benalmádena one of Southern Spain's hottest nightspots.

Benalmádena is made up of three different districts. Cosmopolitan Benalmádena Costa is the main tourist centre and is focused around three main areas of entertainment – Bonanza Square, 24-Hour Square and the Marina – together offering any number of things to see and do.

Further inland, tucked into the foothills of the Sierra de Mijas, Benalmádena Pueblo is the old part of town – the original Andalucían white village, still full of rural charm. Its sleepy, narrow streets and twisting alleyways of white-painted houses with terracotta-tiled roofs present a complete contrast to the hectic pace of the coastal strip. The main square, Plaza de España, contains the statue that has become the symbol of Benalmádena – a young girl offering water in an upturned shell.

Midway between the Pueblo and the coastline, lies the main residential district, called Arroyo de la Miel (meaning 'stream of honey'). It is a busy, fashionable area, with hundreds of apartment blocks and many popular restaurants, bars and clubs. Tivoli World, the resort's top children's attraction, is here, and on Fridays, the local market provides a good opportunity to buy cheap provisions and local handicrafts.

THINGS TO SEE & DO
Auditorio de Benalmádena (Benalmádena Auditorium) ★★
Enjoy theatre, music and dance at the town's grand auditorium located next to the Parque de la Paloma. Events run throughout the year, including a festival at the end of July. ❸ Avenida Antonio Marchada
❶ 952 44 06 40

Puerto Deportivo (see page 38)

Boat trips ★★

Take a boat to see dolphins or go on an organized mini-cruise. Some boat companies combine the trip with a visit to the Sea Life aquarium and a mini-train ride at a special rate. Ask your holiday representative for details.

Castillo Bil-Bil ★

You'll spot this eye-catching crenellated Moorish building in bright reddish-pink towards the western end of the seafront. Formerly a private house, it has been converted into a gallery for temporary exhibitions. It is decorated with tiles and Arabic bas-reliefs. ⓐ Avda Antonio Machado 78 ⓘ 952 44 43 20 ⓞ Open 10.00–13.00, 15.00–20.00 ⓘ Admission charge

Golf ★★

Benalmádena's challenging 18-hole **Torrequebrada Golf Course**, lying a short distance from town in the hills, has a reputation for being a 'thinking person's course'. ⓐ Carretera N340, Km 220 Urb. Torrequebrada ⓘ 952 44 27 42

RESORTS

Horse trekking ★★
Trekking in the hills on a half-day guided excursion, ending with a barbecue back at the riding school. There's a restaurant and children's play area too. **Club Hípico de Benalmádena**. ⓐ Finca Villa Vieja, Urb. Torrequebrada Norte ⓣ 952 56 84 84 ⓦ www.clubhipico.com

Motomercado ★
It's great fun to explore the region by bike or scooter, but remember to take great care. ⓐ Avenida de Alay ⓣ 952 44 11 31 ⓦ www.rentabike.org

Museo de Cultura Precolombina ★★
This charming little museum in the old village contains an interesting collection of pre-Conquest South American artefacts, and some local antiquities, including tiles from an 18th-century shipwreck.
ⓐ Benalmádena Pueblo, Avenida Juan Luis Peralta 49 ⓣ 952 44 85 93
ⓛ Open Tues–Sat 09.30–13.30, 18.00–20.00 (summer); 17.00–19.00 (winter) ⓘ Admission charge

Puerto Deportivo ★★
Looking more like a giant wedding cake than a marina, the Puerto Deportivo complex, with its countless open-air bars, restaurants and clubs, really comes to life at night. There is even underwater lighting.

Sea Life Acuario (Aquarium) ★
This small aquarium with its walk-through water-tunnel, touch-tanks, and feeding demonstrations offers children an unforgettable adventure.
ⓐ Puerto Deportivo ⓣ 952 56 01 50 ⓛ Open 10.00–midnight
ⓘ Admission charge

Telecabina (Cable-car) ★★
Go to the mountains for wonderful sights – it's a 15-minute ride to the summit, from where you can walk down. ⓐ Arroyo de la Miel, near Tivoli
ⓣ 952 57 50 38 ⓛ Open 10.30–01.00 (summer); 10.30–21.30 (winter).

BENALMÁDENA COSTA

SHOPPING

Andycraft Ethnic imports from South East Asia. ⓐ Dársena de Levante, Local 7, Puerto Deportivo ❶ 952 57 41 53

La Artesanía Española Spanish handicrafts, including ceramics, candles and olive wood ⓐ 12 Avda Antonio Machado

Artesanía Piel Interesting leather goods. ⓐ Puerto Deportivo

La Maison en Fleur Souvenirs and presents, including tasteful flower bouquets in silk and paper ⓐ Dársena de Levante, Local Puerto Deportivo A12 ❶ 952 56 02 99

Tivoli World Amusement Park ★★★

Wild West entertainment, with flamenco shows, fairground rides.
ⓐ Avenida Tivoli ❶ 952 57 70 16 ⓦ www.tivolicostadelsol.com
🕐 Open times vary throughout they year; open until 03.00 (July–Aug)
ⓘ Admission charge

BEACHES

Benalmádena boasts 9 km (5.5 miles) of beaches to the west of the new marina – some sandy, some shingle, some artificial – but they are all clean and safe for swimming (**Playa Santa Ana** even has a European Blue Flag for cleanliness). **Playa Las Yucas**, between Hotel Torrequebrada and Hotel Costa Azul, is a nudist beach.

RESTAURANTS AND BARS

Bella Vista €€ Civilized Italian restaurant with a terrace overlooking the marina. ⓐ Puerto Deportivo ❶ 952 44 32 12
🕐 Open Tues–Sun noon–15.30, 19.00–midnight

Bodega de Olé €€ A peaceful, Spanish-style bar run by Brits, with a shady terrace, fine wines and Spanish beers.
ⓐ Plaza Olé

RESORTS

Casa del Gelato € Chill out on the waterfront with delicious home-made ices in fresh fruit flavours such as green apple and mango; some are sugar-free, and there is friendly service. ⓐ Puerto Deportivo ⓣ 952 56 61 07

Chino Internacíonal € Always crowded with locals, this Chinese restaurant has an extensive menu and is excellent value. ⓐ Avenida de la Estación 5, Arroyo de la Miel ⓣ 952 56 12 77 ⓞ Open daily until late

Club de Buceo Los Delfines € The popular little canteen attached to the diving school by the harbour offers unpretentious, perfectly fresh fish and good tapas. There are tables outside, and friendly service. Excellent value. ⓐ Puerto Deportivo ⓣ 952 44 09 89 ⓞ Open 13.00–16.30, 20.30–midnight

El Elefante € Wholesome English home cooking accompanied by various raucous entertainments seven nights a week, including cabaret, hypnotists. ⓐ Benalmádena Plaza. ⓣ 952 56 22 46 ⓞ Open 20.00–01.00

Mar de Alboran €€€ One of the smartest restaurants in town, near the entrance to the port, offering accomplished modern cooking with a decent wine list. A menu of the day gives you a chance to sample the chef's best efforts. ⓐ Avenida de Alay 5 ⓣ 952 44 64 27 ⓞ Closed Sun eve and Mon (winter); closed Sun eve (summer)

El Mero €€€ Sophisticated fish restaurant with a cool terrace overhanging the port. Try the bream baked in salt. ⓐ Dársena de Levante, Puerto Marina ⓣ 952 44 07 52 ⓞ Open 13.00–01.00

The Office €€ Run by a British couple, this lively place is popular with UK visitors. Hearty cooked breakfasts, traditional Sunday lunches and plenty of daily specials. ⓐ Calle Salvador Allende ⓣ 952 38 67 43 ⓞ Open Fri–Wed 09.00–midnight

BENALMÁDENA COSTA

Restaurante La Sirena €€ A bustling seafront restaurant beside the port. Specialities include fresh seafood and braised meats.
ⓐ Playa de Santa Ana 8 ⓣ 952 56 01 62

El Varadero €€ A harbourside restaurant with a friendly atmosphere and a good range of local meat and seafood dishes.
ⓐ Puerto Deportivo ⓣ 952 56 43 27

Ventorillo de la Perra €€€ A very typical Spanish restaurant. Both local Malagueño cooking and general Spanish fare.
ⓐ Avenida Constitución 115, Arroyo de la Miel ⓣ 952 44 19 66
ⓛ Open Tues–Sun 13.00–15.00, 19.30–23.30

NIGHTLIFE

Bar Maracas Samba the night away at this buzzing nightspot. Arrive before midnight as queues can be long. Be warned – dancing on the bar top is a regular occurence. ⓐ Puerto Deportivo

Casino Torrequebrada Take your passport and try your luck at the tables. Not quite as smart as Marbella, but do dress up. ⓐ Hotel Torrequebrada ⓐ Carretera N340, Km 220 ⓣ 952 44 60 00 ⓛ Open 21.00–05.00

Joy A popular club in the Marina area, attracting locals and visitors alike.
ⓐ Puerto Marina ⓣ 952 56 34 44 ⓛ Open 23.00–06.00 ⓘ Admission charge; Thursday is ladies' night (free entry)

Kiu One of the biggest discos in town, with three DJs and three dance floors, all playing different types of music. ⓐ Plaza Solymar (just off 24-Hour Square) ⓣ 952 44 05 18 ⓛ Open 23.00–06.30 (until 07.30 Fri and Sat) ⓘ Admission charge

Sala de Fiestas Fortuna Hotel Torrequebrada's cabaret act is a spectacular show. ⓐ Carretera N340, Km 220 ⓣ 95 2446000 ⓛ Tues–Sat 10.30–00.30 ⓘ Admission charge includes dinner and entry to the Casino

RESORTS

Torremolinos is a world-famous resort

TORREMOLINOS

Torremolinos
good-time resort

The tourist boom of the 1950s, which made the Costa del Sol a world-famous holiday destination, all began in Torremolinos – a tiny fishing village turned big, brash resort. Few places in southern Spain can offer as many hotels, bars and discos and, for sun-worshippers, 'Torrie' offers some of the best beaches on the coast.

It once had a reputation for being a downmarket resort, but recently it has shaken off this 'Terrible Torrie' image by smartening up the town and building an elegant beach promenade. By night, the neon-lit streets of the attractive old town throng with life until the early hours.

La Carihuela (the westernmost district of the resort) is a reminder of Torrie's humble beginnings as a simple fishing village. Its atmospheric, whitewashed streets are crammed with restaurants, and fishermen still barbecue silvery sardines on wooden skewers on the beach.

THINGS TO SEE & DO
Aquapark ★★
Fun for all the family, with wave machines, a 'water mountain', and the largest water-slide in Europe. ⓐ Carretera de Circunvalacíon (near Palacio de Congresos) ⓣ 952 38 88 88 ⓞ Open 10.00–18.00 (May, June, Sept); 10.00–19.00 (Jul–Aug) ⓘ Admission charge

Crocodile Park ★
You'll be sure of happy snaps for the family album at this fascinating nature park. ⓐ Near Aquapark ⓞ Open 10.00–19.00 (May–Sept); 10.00–17.00 (Oct–Apr) ⓘ Admission charge

El Ranchito ★★
If you are unable to get to Jerez to see the dancing horses, come here to this similar but smaller show. ⓐ Senda del Pilar 4 ⓣ 952 38 30 63 ⓘ Dressage demonstrations each Wed at 17.45 – book through your hotel.

RESORTS

BEACHES

You can find some of the best beaches of the Costa here, notably the two main beaches of **Playamar** and **Bajondillo**. Then there is **Playa de la Carihuela** fringing Torrie's original fishing village to the west, and the quieter **Playa de los Alamo**s to the east. All have sunbeds, umbrellas and pedalos to rent, as well as showers, café-bars and restaurants. At the height of summer, there are often beach volleyball and football competitions. Water sports are available at nearby Benalmádena marina.

RESTAURANTS

Albahaca €€ A rare vegetarian restaurant on this carniverous coast. This one deserves to do well, with a daily changing four-course menu for less than a round of drinks back home.
ⓐ Doña Maria Barrabino 11 ⓣ 952 37 51 82 ⓛ Open Mon–Sat 20.30–23.30

Cunard Bar €€ Looking for a taste of home? Head here for hearty home cooking; run by a Welsh family. ⓐ Calle Bulto, La Carihuela ⓣ 952 05 09 07 ⓛ Open Fri–Wed 20.00–midnight

Frutos €€€ A great place for spotting celebrities. ⓐ Carretera N340, Km 228 ⓣ 952 38 14 50 ⓛ Closed Sun eve

El Molino de la Torre €€ Good-value restaurant with striking sea views from the roof terrace. ⓐ Calle Cuesta del Tajo 8 ⓣ 952 38 77 56 ⓛ Open 19.00–23.00

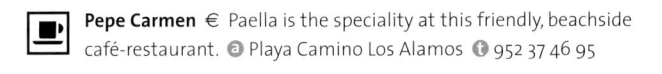

Pepe Carmen € Paella is the speciality at this friendly, beachside café-restaurant. ⓐ Playa Camino Los Alamos ⓣ 952 37 46 95

Shang-Hai € Cheap, cheerful Chinese restaurant. ⓐ Avenida Lido 15, Nuevo Playamar ⓣ 952 37 57 44 ⓛ Open daily till late

A bewildering number of bars and restaurants line La Carihuela's long seafront. Some of the best include **Casa Guaquin** (ⓛ closed Mon) and its

TORREMOLINOS

> ### SHOPPING
>
> **Cortefiel** It's easy to pick up a bargain in this fashionable clothes store, especially during the summer sales.
> ⓐ Avenida Palma de Mallorca ⓣ 952 37 02 12 ⓞ Open Mon–Sat
> **Lepanto** Superb patisserie. Try the strawberry tartlets or homemade mango ice cream. ⓐ Calle San Miguel 54 ⓣ 952 38 66 29
> **Licorería San Miguel** Great for Spanish wines, brandies and liqueurs. ⓐ Calle San Miguel 43 ⓣ 952 38 33 13 ⓞ Open Mon–Sat

neighbour **El Roqueo** (closed Tues), at Calle Carmen 35 and 37. **Casa Juan** (closed Mon) and **La Jábega** are both on Calle del Mar at 14 and 17. For a fishy snack, try one of its typical *chiringuitos* (beachside café-bars). Two good ones are **Isabel** and **El Canarias Playa**.

NIGHTLIFE

Eugenios A long-established disco in 'Torrole', one of the last remaining clubs in the Pueblo Blanco area. ⓐ Calle Case Blanca 22 ⓣ 952 38 11 31

Palladium Regularly packed solid with visitors, dancing to the latest rave sounds. ⓐ Avenida Palma de Mallorca 36 ⓣ 952 38 42 89 ⓞ Open 23.00–06.00 ⓘ Admission charge

Pepe Lopez Touristic but popular flamenco shows. ⓐ Plaza de la Gamba Alegre ⓣ 952 38 12 84 ⓞ Open Mon–Sat ⓘ Show runs 22.30–00.30

Veronia Music ranges from Sevillanas to the latest chart toppers at this bopping night club near the centre of town. ⓐ Avda Salvador Allende 10 ⓣ 952 37 24 70 ⓞ Open 23.00–late

Voltage Dance the night away to all the latest tunes. ⓐ Avda Palma de Mallorca ⓞ Open 22.00–06.00

RESORTS

Nerja
mountains and caves

Nerja (pronounced 'nair-ha') is the jewel of the eastern Costa del Sol. Its tranquil, whitewashed streets and typical Andalucían houses, adorned with splashy scarlet geraniums in terracotta pots, retain much of its ancient Moorish character as well as offering visitors fabulous beaches and all the facilities of an international resort. The old town is centred on the Balcón de Europa – all the cobbled streets and alleyways radiate outward from here, full of cafés and tiny boutiques. By night they are twinkling with fairy lights and alive with tapas bars and restaurants.

THINGS TO SEE & DO
Balcón de Europa (Balcony of Europe) ★★★
This magnificent palm-lined promenade sits atop a cliff, providing dazzling views. It marks the start of a scenic path that winds its way over the rocks bordering the shore to Burriana Beach. Horse and carriage tours also leave from here, taking in most of Nerja's sights.

Cuevas de Nerja (Caves of Nerja) ★★★
One of the most visited sights in Spain – vast prehistoric caverns here contain a fairytale world of magically lit stalactites and stalagmites. One cave, containing Stone Age paintings and the largest stalactite in the world, has been dubbed the 'Cathedral of the Costa del Sol'. ⓐ Carretera Maro ⓘ 952 52 95 20 ⓒ Open daily ⓘ Admission charge

EXCURSIONS
Almuñecar ★
A popular destination with Spaniards from the Granada area. The outskirts are rather built up, but it has a few interesting sights (such as Roman and Phoenician remains), good, if greyish, beaches and lots of lively bars and restaurants. Make for the old town around the Plaza Ayuntamiento for good tapas. From the coastal highway, a picturesque mountain road winds its way through the mountains to Granada.

NERJA

> **SHOPPING**
>
> Every Tuesday morning, the streets of Nerja come alive for the weekly market – worth a stop, as are these:
> **Creaciones Guacamayo** Costume jewellery in a kaleidoscopic range of semiprecious stones. ⓐ Calle El Barrio 4 ⓣ 952 52 15 30
> **Licorería Arce** Wines, spirits, liqueurs and tobacco products.
> ⓐ Calle Pintada 7 ⓣ 952 52 81 21 ⓔ licoreriaarce@Nerja.net
> **Manos** Handmade leatherware, jewellery, pottery and other goodies. ⓐ Calle Pintada ⓣ 952 52 11 37/8 ⓞ Open Mon–Sat

Frigiliana ★★★
A visit to the nearby sleepy hilltop village of Frigiliana, with its cobbled alleyways and pristine white houses, splashed with geraniums and bougainvillea is a must. Frigiliana has been awarded the title of 'Prettiest village in Andalucía' and is famous for its pottery and sweet wine.

Maro ★★
The pretty village of Maro, 4 km (2 miles) east of Nerja, enjoys lovely views from its church square over a sandy cove. Look out for the aqueduct on the other side of the main road near the turn-off to the village.

Salobreña ★★★
A spectacular Moorish castle dominates this attractive town surrounded by sugar-cane plantations. At the foot of the hill is a 16th-century church.

BEACHES
Playa Calahonda, a fishermen's beach, and **Playa El Salón** are nearest to the town. **Playa Torrecilla** to the west is larger and less crowded, but the best beach is **Playa Burriana** (20 minutes' walk on the coastal footpath to the east) with excellent facilities, lively bars and restaurants. **Club Náutique Nerja** has details of diving, sailing, mountain biking, riding and guided walks. ⓐ Avda Castilla Pérez 2 ⓣ 952 52 46 54

RESORTS

RESTAURANTS & BARS

Antonio €€ Waterfront restaurant serving fish and tapas.
ⓐ Paseo Marítimo 12, Almuñecar ⓣ 958 63 00 20

La Bodega €€ Authentic wine bar stacked with barrels. ⓐ Plaza La Marina ⓣ 952 52 52 04 ⓛ Open Thurs–Tues 20.00–23.00

Casa Luque €€€ Elegant dining in lovely gardens overlooking the sea. ⓐ Plaza Canavas 2 ⓣ 952 52 10 04

Casa Maro €€ Delightful restaurant in an eccentric old house in a lovely quiet spot near the church. ⓐ Calle Maro ⓣ 952 52 52 04

Casa Paco € Velilla seafront east of the town, famed for seafood and caramel custard ⓐ Playa Velilla, Almuñecar ⓣ 958 63 10 51

Chiringuito El Peñón €€ Super location on a rocky promontory just above the waves. Fish and meat barbecue every evening in summer. ⓐ Playa del Peñón, Salobreña ⓣ 958 61 05 38

The Cottage €€ An attractive terrace and garden make this a popular English-run place. ⓐ Calle Cristo 68 ⓣ 952 52 54 92

Don Comer € Sandwiches and snacks at this popular local.
ⓐ Calle Granada ⓣ 952 52 60 06 ⓛ Open Thurs–Tues

The Garden Restaurant €€€ A well-established place in a wonderful setting. ⓐ Frigiliana ⓣ 952 53 31 85

Haveli € A lively and popular Indian Tandoori restaurant.
ⓐ Calle Cristo 44 ⓣ 952 52 42 97 ⓛ Open til late

Marisquería La Marina € The freshest seafood tapas in town.
ⓐ Plaza la Marina ⓣ 952 52 12 99

De Miguel €€€ One of Nerja's smartest eating places. ⓐ Calle Pintada 2, near the tourist office ⓣ 952 52 29 96

The Rendezvous €€ An English restaurant serving family-orientated menus and good vegetarian options in beautiful surroundings. ⓐ Calle Almirante Ferrandiz ⓘ Booking essential.

La Strada € Authentic pizzas cooked in a wood-burning stove. Takeaway. ⓐ Calle Chaparil 5 ⓣ 952 52 30 88 ⓞ Open Thurs–Tues

Verano Azul €€ A smart, lively place serving good Spanish dishes – lots of tables outside. ⓐ Calle Almirante Ferrandiz 31

NIGHTLIFE

Blanco y Negro This monochrome action-packed nightspot offers a mix of live entertainment and televised sport. ⓐ Calle Pintada 35

Buena Sombre A great bar for people-watching. ⓐ Plaza Tutti Frutti

El Burro Blanco Live flamenco and international music. ⓐ Calle Gloria

El Colono One of the top flamenco spots in town. ⓐ Calle Granada 6 ⓣ 952 52 18 26 ⓞ Dinner shows Wed and Fri ⓘ Cash only

Jimmy's Nerja's biggest nightclub attracts a young, trendy crowd. ⓐ Calle Antonio Millón ⓞ Open midnight–07.00 ⓘ Admission charge

Narisa Sophisticated, popular night club. ⓐ Balcón de Europa ⓣ 952 52 68 46 ⓞ Open 01.00–08.00 ⓘ Admission charge

Pub Rio Dance under the stars in this tropical style open air disco. ⓐ Rambla del Rio Chillar. ⓞ July–Sept midnight–07.00.

Pub Taebas A place to relax over a cold beer. ⓐ Plaza Tutti Frutti

Almerimar – an oasis in the Costa de Almería

Almerimar
fast-growing resort

The Costa de Almería begins east of Motril, and the scenery takes on a ghostly pallor. Pale, desiccated hills loom inland, while vast expanses of plastic horticultural sheeting stretch over the coastal plains, sheltering prodigious quantities of intensively grown fruit and salad vegetables – strawberries, peppers, cucumbers, melons. The sheer scale of the enterprise is awesome. This is one section of the coast where agricultural land is still more valuable than building plots. Much of the produce grown in the makeshift hothouses around El Ejido ends up in British supermarket trolleys.

But there's more to the Costa de Almería than market gardening. The fast highway that slices arrow-straight across the Campo de Dalías bypasses an apron of coastal plain containing several fast-growing

ALMERIMAR

resorts. None of these places has anything like the high profile of, say, Torremolinos or Marbella. But visitors to these little-known areas may be pleasantly surprised by the long expanses of unspoilt beach on their doorsteps. The region also lays claim to an unexpectedly wild and watery world of reedbeds and saltmarsh lagoons, haunt of migrant flamingos and huge dragonflies. Amid these contrasting landscapes, the gleaming designer-built marina resort of Almerimar erupts like a strange space-station oasis. Fringed by an immaculate golf course as well as an approach-drive aglow with pink oleander, its state-of-the-art quaysides bristle with shops, restaurants and bars. Glass-bottomed boat trips and sub-aqua activities make the most of the clear, warm water.

RESTAURANTS

Heladería Cafetería Noray € Ice creams and fruit juices, along with other drinks. Spacious waterfront terrace. ⓐ Dársena 3, Puerto Deportivo ⓣ 950 49 75 53 ⓞ Open Sat–Thurs til 23.30

El Náutico €€€ One of the prettiest of Almerimar's waterfront buildings, in Moorish Andalucían style with terrace tables outside. Specialities include clams, carpaccio, partridge in vinegar. ⓐ Dársena 1, Puerto Deportivo ⓣ 950 49 71 62 ⓞ Open 19.30–23.30

El Segoviano €€ Traditional Castilian cooking, including suckling pig. ⓐ Dársena 2, Puerto Deportivo ⓣ 950 49 75 44 ⓞ Open Mon–Sat 20.00–23.00

NIGHTLIFE

Edificio Jaleo Literally meaning 'stir it up', this complex houses a number of clubs and is a good bet for a night on the dance floor. ⓐ Dársena 1, Paseo Poniente ⓞ Open till late

Taberna La Soleá Popular bar with music and good tapas, especially locally cured hams and cheeses. ⓐ Centro Comercial la Estrella, Dársena 2, Puerto Deportivo ⓣ 950 49 76 01 ⓞ Open Tues–Sun

RESORTS

Roquetas
a touch of style

Roquetas is a surprisingly populous area, a former fishing port recently expanded by the burgeoning horti-business of intensive cultivation under plastic that occupies many acres of the local hinterland. Many of the workers who service this greenhouse empire live in Roquetas town. The newer resort of Roquetas de Mar lies some way south west of the town (follow signs to 'Urbanizaciones' or 'Roquetas Costa').

Architecturally, Roquetas is an unusual place. Avoiding the stark high-rises that have fallen out of favour on many parts of the Mediterranean coast, Roquetas has opted for a stylish brand of Andalucían post-modernism – all fantasy turrets and uneven rooflines. Certainly it is more attractive and interesting to look at than many modern resorts. Accommodation has an upmarket air, and there's a mix of nationalities, including German and Belgian visitors. The long seafront encompasses several town beaches, but the main resort strand is **Playa Serena**, a Blue Flag beach.

THINGS TO SEE & DO
Mariopark ★
A jolly water park promising family fun with Black Holes, kamikaze slides and toboggans. ❸ Camino Las Salinas ❶ 950 32 75 75 ❹ Open 11.00–19.00, closed winter ❶ Admission charge

Punta Entinas–Sabinar ★★
The peaceful saltmarsh habitats between Roquetas de Mar's Playa Serena and Almerimar are now a protected nature reserve and a paradise for wildlife and birdwatchers. Over 200 species of birds can be found in a 16 km (10 mile) coastal strip of lagoons and reedbeds, including flamingos at certain times of year. Unusual plants, insects, lizards and toads also live in the marshes.

ROQUETAS

Sail & Surf Roquetas ★
Windsurfing and sailing fans are well catered for, with equipment hire and tuition, on Playa Serena, by **Sail & Surf Roquetas**. ⓐ In front of Hotel Bahía Serena ⓘ 630 55 23 85 (mobile)

RESTAURANTS & BARS

La Alpujarra €€ A good bet for a light meal at any time of day. ⓐ Urb. Playa Serena (near Hotel Golf Trinidad) ⓘ 950 33 38 59

Cafetería Balix € Spanning the cultural divides, this agreeable little place obliges with German, English or Spanish-style breakfasts and much else besides. Central and friendly. ⓐ Urb. Playa Serena

Cha-Cha € This South-American style bar packs them in at weekends and has a Latin vibe. ⓐ Edificio Los Flamencos, Playa Serena

Chino Shanghai € Good-value lunch menu and over 100 oriental favourites. ⓐ Avenida del Mediterráneo

Heladería Alicante € Mouth-watering range of ice creams and cakes to eat in or take away. ⓐ Avenida del Mediterráneo

Suzi's €€ A small, neat tapas bar serving a range of seafood snacks (smoked sardines, small clams, etc). Also hot dogs and black pudding. Tables outside. ⓐ Avda Playa Serena

NIGHTLIFE
Disco Feeling One of the brightest nightspots in town, with regular themed party nights. ⓐ Urb. Playa Serena

---

The flattish terrain of Roquetas makes pedal bikes or *carros* (a sort of giant, four-wheeled tandem with room for all the family) a popular way of getting around.

RESORTS

Aguadulce
simple beachside fun

The oldest of the three Costa de Almería resorts, the quieter Aguadulce has more traditional-looking hotels and apartment blocks well interspersed with greenery along its pleasant palm-lined seafront. Mostly a family resort, the port area livens up in the evenings. The long beach is meticulously combed by machines in the early mornings.

La Puebla del Vicar, just off the N340 a few kilometres west of Aguadulce, holds a colourful Sunday morning market selling anything and everything. Local ceramics, leatherware, fruit and nuts – and a good line in plastic fly-swats. Don't confuse this place with the pretty village called Vicar, further inland.

RESTAURANTS

Asador Castelao €€ One of the most accomplished restaurants in the port. Galician specialities such as *zarzuelas* (fish casseroles), *empanadas* (filled pasties) and good seafood. ⓐ Puerto Deportivo ⓘ 950 34 34 62 ⓒ Closed Mon mornings

La Cueva €€ A mix of Spanish cuisine: paella, fish and meat dishes and local sausages and hams. ⓐ Puerto Deportivo ⓘ 950 34 72 89

La Gruta €€€ This excellent restaurant in a cave overlooking the sea, specializes in grilled meats, and has a good wine list. ⓐ Some distance out of town above the Almería road, Carretera N340, Km 436; watch carefully for the turn-off ⓘ 950 23 93 35 ⓒ Closed Sun and the first two weeks of Oct and Feb

El Paladar € Smart green decor here, with a mix of ice creams, pizzas by the yard and decent tapas. ⓐ Puerto Deportivo, Ribera 7, at the west end of the port ⓘ 950 34 48 57

EXCURSIONS
Out & about

EXCURSIONS

Sevilla
vibrant city

Sevilla (Seville) is the capital of Andalucía, Spain's fourth city, and one of its most exciting. Majestic, lively and passionately Spanish, it is the home of *Carmen*, *Don Juan* and the cradle of flamenco. As a local saying goes: 'he who hasn't seen Sevilla, has seen no wondrous thing.'

Sevilla is easy to explore on foot, with most of the main sights clustered alongside or near the Guadalquivir river. Be sure to visit the picturesque Santa Cruz district east of the cathedral, with its narrow streets of white-washed buildings, shaded squares and flower-filled patios, and Triana, across the river, especially popular at night with its countless tapas bars and tiny restaurants. It is here that flamenco is said to have been created, and for many Triana is still *the* place in Spain to experience spontaneous flamenco and *sevillanas* dancing.

THINGS TO SEE & DO
Antigua Fábrica de Tabacos (Old Tobacco Factory) ★★
The 18th-century tobacco factory is where the beautiful gypsy Carmen from Bizet's opera worked as a cigar maker, before being stabbed to death by her lover. It is now part of the university and is not open to the public, but the exterior is stunning. ⓐ Calle San Fernando

GETTING ABOUT
Open-top bus tours are a great way to see the city. Buses leave half-hourly from the Torre del Oro by the river, and cover all the main sites. **Sevirama bus tours** ⓐ Torre del Oro ⓣ 954 56 06 93
A romantic way to see the sights, hour-long river cruises run daily every 30 minutes from 11.00 to 22.00 from the quayside below the Torre del Oro. Also a night-time cruise (*crucero de noche*) with an on-board fiesta. **Cruceros Turísticos** ⓐ Torre del Oro ⓣ 954 21 13 96

Seville Map

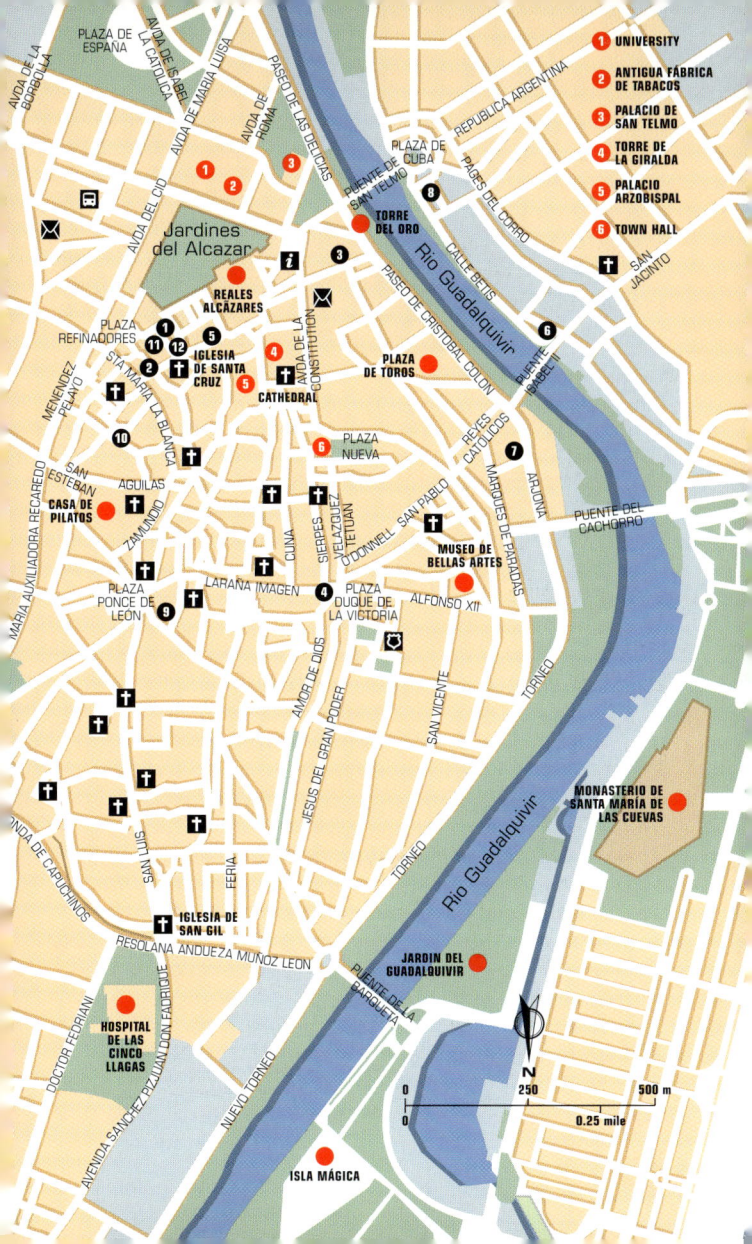

Legend
1. UNIVERSITY
2. ANTIGUA FÁBRICA DE TABACOS
3. PALACIO DE SAN TELMO
4. TORRE DE LA GIRALDA
5. PALACIO ARZOBISPAL
6. TOWN HALL

Labeled Locations

Plazas and Squares:
- Plaza de España
- Plaza de la Gavidia
- Plaza de Cuba
- Plaza Refinadores
- Plaza de Toros
- Plaza Nueva
- Plaza Duque de la Victoria
- Plaza Ponce de León

Monuments and Buildings:
- Jardines del Alcazar
- Reales Alcázares
- Torre del Oro
- Iglesia de Santa Cruz
- Cathedral
- Casa de Pilatos
- Museo de Bellas Artes
- Iglesia de San Gil
- Hospital de las Cinco Llagas
- Monasterio de Santa María de las Cuevas
- Jardin del Guadalquivir
- Isla Mágica
- San Jacinto

Streets and Avenues:
- Avda. de la Borbolla
- Avda. de Isabel la Católica
- Avda. de María Luisa
- Avda. de Roma
- Paseo de las Delicias
- Avda. del Cid
- República Argentina
- Pagés del Corro
- Calle Betis
- Avda. de la Constitución
- Paseo de Cristóbal Colón
- Reyes Católicos
- Marqués de Paradas
- Arjona
- Menéndez Pelayo
- Sta. María la Blanca
- San Esteban
- Aguilas
- Zamudio
- Sierpes
- Cuna
- Velázquez
- Tetuán
- O'Donnell
- San Pablo
- Laraña
- Imagen
- Alfonso XII
- Amor de Dios
- Jesús del Gran Poder
- San Vicente
- Torneo
- Feria
- San Luis
- Resolana
- Andueza
- Muñoz León
- Doctor Fedriani
- María Auxiliadora
- Recaredo
- Avenida Sánchez Pizjuán
- Don Fadrique
- Nuevo Torneo

Bridges:
- Puente de San Telmo
- Puente Isabel II
- Puente del Cachorro
- Puente de la Barqueta

Río Guadalquivir

Scale: 0 — 250 — 500 m / 0 — 0.25 mile

EXCURSIONS

Casa de Pilatos (Pilate's House) ★★
Pilate's House is one of Sevilla's finest palaces, dating from the early 1500s. A Renaissance façade conceals typical Moorish courtyard gardens containing classical statues and lovely Mudéjar ceilings. ⓐ Plaza de Pilatos 1 ⓣ 954 22 52 98 ⓞ Ground floor open 09.00–19.00 (summer); 09.00–18.00 (winter). First floor open 10.00–14.00, 15.00–19.00 (summer); 10.00–14.00, 15.00–18.00 (winter) ⓘ Admission charge

Cathedral ★★★
This is the largest Gothic cathedral in the world. It took 104 years to build, and contains a staggering 43 chapels. The high altar alone (also the largest in the world!) took 82 years to complete. Christopher Columbus's (alleged) tomb lies in the southern aisle. ⓐ Avda de la Constitucion ⓣ 957 56 33 21 ⓞ Open Mon–Sat 10.30–18.00, Sun 10.00–13.30, 14.00–16.00 ⓘ Admission charge (combined with Giralda)

Isla Mágica ★★
This fantasy theme park on the Expo 92 exhibition site takes you back four centuries to the discovery of the New World, with spectacular multi-media presentations based on the adventures of the explorers. ⓐ Pabellón de España, Isla de la Cartuja ⓣ 902 16 17 16 ⓦ www.Islamagica.es ⓞ Open mid-Mar–early Dec 11.00–23.00 (summer with seasonal variations); 11.00–22.00 (winter) ⓘ Admission charge

Museo de Bellas Artes (Fine Arts Museum) ★★★
In a former convent, this houses an important collection of Sevillian baroque masterpieces, including works by Murillo, Zurbarán and Juan de Mesa, and is one of the major galleries of the country. ⓐ Plaza del Museo 9 ⓣ 954 22 07 90 ⓞ Open Tues 15.00–20.00, Wed–Sat 09.00–20.00, Sun 09.00–14.00 ⓘ Admission free with EU passport

Plaza de España ★★
Constructed for a major exhibition in 1929, this monumental semicircular plaza on the east side of the city is one of Sevilla's most

> **SHOPPING**
>
> The best area for shopping is the Centro, or central zone, which lies north of the cathedral at the heart of the city, around Plaza Nueva, Plaza Duque de la Victoria and chic, pedestrianized Calle Sierpes. The latter is lined with enticing boutiques of clothes and jewellery and window displays of fans, hats, shawls and flamenco dresses.

striking public spaces, featuring grandly towered buildings, fountain pools and bright ceramic tiles representing all Spain's 51 provinces.

Reales Alcázares (Royal Fortress) ★★★
This magnificent 14th-century Muslim fortress is one of the best surviving examples of Moorish architecture in Europe and not to be missed. It also has beautiful gardens. ⓐ Plaza del Triunfo, Puerta del Leon ⓐ 954 56 00 40 ⓐ Open Tues–Sat 09.30–20.00, Sun and hols 09.30–18.00 (Apr–Sept); Tues–Sat 09.30–18.00, Sun and hols 09.30–14.30 (Oct–Mar) ⓐ Admission charge

Torre de la Giralda (Giralda Tower) ★★★
This is the tallest tower in Spain, a 70 m (230 ft)-high minaret – the only remaining feature of the city's ancient Moorish temple. ⓐ Plaza Virgen de los Reyes ⓐ 954 56 33 21 ⓐ For opening times, see Cathedral, page 58 ⓐ Admission charge

Torre del Oro (Golden Tower) ★★
The Moorish 'Golden Tower', built in 1220 to guard the Guadalquivir river, was originally covered in golden tiles and linked to a second 'Silver Tower' by a large chain. Today this impressive 12-sided building houses a small maritime museum. ⓐ Paseo de Cristóbal Colón ⓐ 954 22 24 19 ⓐ Open Tues–Fri 10.00–14.00, Sat and Sun 11.00–14.00 (closed Aug) ⓐ Admission charge (free Tues)

EXCURSIONS

RESTAURANTS (see map on page 57)

La Albahaca €€€ ❶ Set in a typical Andalucían house with terrace, this elegant restaurant is a favourite with Sevillanos.
ⓐ Plaza de Santa Cruz 12 ⓣ 954 22 07 14 ⓛ Open Mon–Sat 13.00–16.00, 20.00–midnight

Altamira €€ ❷ An enjoyable café for people-watching with tables set on the square of Santa María la Blanca. Plenty of daytime and evening ambience, and a few serenading minstrels.
ⓐ Calle Santa María la Blanca 6 ⓣ 954 42 50 30 ⓛ Open daily

Bodegón Torre del Oro €€ ❸ Well-known haunt for evening tapas and good-value set menus, near the Golden Tower. Try *urta*, a local fish. ⓐ Postigo del Carbon 15 ⓣ 954 22 08 80 ⓛ Open Mon–Fri 07.00–01.00, Sat–Sun 12.30–23.30

Confitería La Campaña €€ ❹ A legendary cake shop at the beginning of Calle Sierpes serving snacks, drinks and ices at a few pavement tables. *Turrón* (flavoured nougat), crystallized fruit and picnic food on sale inside, besides the luscious cakes. ⓐ Calle Sierpes 1–3
ⓣ 954 22 35 70

Hosteria del Laurel €€ ❺ This is a lovely old inn with a tiled tapas bar in the heart of Santa Cruz. ⓐ Plaza de los Venerables 5 ⓣ 954 22 02 95 ⓦ www.hosteriadellalaurel.com
ⓛ Open daily

Kiosko de las Flores € ❻ A splendid old-fashioned little *freiduría* (fried fish shop) near the Puente Isabel II, specializing in fried fish and clams. ⓐ Calle Betis ⓣ 954 27 45 76

La Mandragora € ❼ One of very few vegetarian restaurants in town. ⓐ Calle Albuera 11 ⓣ 954 22 01 84 ⓛ Open for lunch Tues–Sat, dinner Thur–Sat; closed Sun and Mon.

Ox's €€ ❽ A highly regarded *asador* (grill-room) on the Triana riverbank. Basque fish specialities and steaks. ⓐ Calle Betis 61 ⓣ 954 27 62 75 ⓞ Open Mon– Sat 13.30–15.30, 20.30–midnight

El Rinconcillo €€ ❾ Dating back to the 17th century and one of the best tapas bars in town. ⓐ Calle Gerona 42 ⓣ 954 22 31 83 ⓞ Open Thurs–Tues

NIGHTLIFE

Besides its famous tapas bars and *terrazas de verano* (open-air music bars set up temporarily along the waterfront in summer), Sevilla has many other nightspots. Calle Betis (Triana waterfront) livens up as the evening progresses, while the cafés and bars near Santa María la Blanca make an ideal spot for watching the world go by. Some of the flamenco shows on offer in Sevilla are very touristy. Try local bars for these typical *sevillanas* evenings instead; some make no extra charge for music.

▲ *Plaza de España, Sevilla*

La Carbonería ❿ Renowned music bar for flamenco, blues and rock, tucked away in back streets in former coal merchant's premises. Livens up late; best on Monday and Thursday. ⓐ Calle Levíes 18 ⓣ 954 21 44 60

Los Gallos ⓫ One of the top flamenco shows in town. ⓐ Plaza de Santa Cruz ⓣ 954 21 69 81 ⓦ www.tablaolosgallos.com ⓞ Performances at 21.00 and 23.30 ⓘ Admission charge

El Tamboril ⓬ Popular Santa Cruz bar with impromptu flamenco shows and midnight rumba. ⓐ Plaza de Santa Cruz

SPAIN
MARINA
NORTH MOLE
DEVIL'S TOWER ROAD
EASTERN BEACH
GRAND CASEMATES SQUARE
MOORISH CASTLE
GREAT SIEGE TUNNELS
QUEENSWAY
LINE WALL RD
MAIN STREET
WILLIS'S ROAD
QUEEN'S ROAD
GIBRALTAR MUSEUM
CATALAN BAY
WATER CATCHMENTS
GOVERNOR'S RESIDENCE
SIR HERBERT MILES ROAD
QUEENSWAY QUAY
CABLE CAR
ALAMEDA GARDENS
SANDY BAY
THE APES' DEN
QUEEN'S ROAD
EUROPA ROAD
ENGINEER ROAD
O'HARAS BATTERY (HIGHEST POINT ON THE ROCK)
ST MICHAEL'S CAVE
ROSIA BAY
GORHAM'S CAVE
VIEWPOINT
CAMP BAY
Bay of Gibraltar
N
LITTLE BAY
EUROPA ROAD
0
500 m
1km
0
0.25 mile
EUROPA POINT

GIBRALTAR

Gibraltar
colonial rock

Gibraltar is a towering chunk of ancient limestone, known as 'The Rock', which guards the narrow entrance to the Mediterranean. Gibraltar Town is very like a British town, but with a suntan. The streets, phone boxes, cars, currency, pubs and shops are all British – but the climate and the beaches are definitely Mediterranean.

You need to show your passport on entering and leaving Gibraltar. Border formalities can be very protracted, especially for motorists. Park in La Línea, on the Spanish side. On Sunday, many shops and sights are closed and the cable car doesn't operate.

THINGS TO SEE & DO
A quick visit to Gibraltar's museum provides an invaluable historic insight before taking the cable car up to the top of the Rock to admire its many sights and the stupendous views. A blanket 'Nature Reserve' charge is made to enter any of the sights at the 'Top of the Rock'. On a guided tour, you can get an all-in deal. Sights are generally open 10.00–19.00 (summer), 10.00–17.30 (winter).

The Apes' Den ★★★
Halfway up the Rock are the famous Barbary apes – the only group of wild primates remaining in Europe. It is said that as long as they are here, Gibraltar will remain British. Hang on carefully to your belongings.

Dolphin watching ★★
Trips to observe three species of dolphins that swim in the bay are available year-round.

Europa Point ★★
On a clear day, you can see Africa from the southernmost point of the Rock – the 'Tip of Europe'. ❶ No admission charge

EXCURSIONS

◐ *View of 'The Rock'*

Great Siege Tunnels ★★
This vast network (48 km/ 29 miles) of tunnels resembling a Swiss cheese were dug into the rock in 1782 so that the British forces could better position their cannons at a great height, thus enabling them to win the Great Siege.

Moorish Castle ★
Only one tower remains of this ancient 8th-century Moorish Castle, where once the people of Gibraltar sheltered and took refuge from marauding pirates who virtually destroyed the town.

St Michael's Cave ★★★
St Michael's Cave is the largest of the group of caves on Gibraltar. Once home to groups of Neolithic people, its dramatic rock formations now provide the backdrop for concerts and fashion shows. Legend has it that there is an underground tunnel in one of the caves that leads under the Straits to Africa.

RESTAURANTS & BARS

Many of the hundreds of traditional pubs in Gibraltar serve excellent pub grub. Try **The Clipper** (78b Irish Town) for hearty Sunday roasts, **Ye Olde Rock** (12 John Mackintosh Square) for Cornish pasties and Guinness and **The Angry Friar** (287 Main Street) for its all-day breakfast. On the waterfront, the Queensway Quay area has some attractive bars and restaurants. The **International Casino** (7 Europa Road) has a terrace restaurant as well as gambling opportunities galore.

SHOPPING

Gibraltar's VAT-free status makes it a popular place for a shopping spree, particularly for perfume, jewellery, alcohol and electronic goods. British high street chains, such as M&S, are much cheaper than in the UK. All shops follow British rather than Spanish opening times, closing at 18.00 hours and opening on Sundays.

For bargains around Main Street, try:

Gibraltar Crystal For fine glassware. ⓐ Grand Casemates Square
The Crown Jewels For jewellery. ⓐ No. 105
Prestige For Lladró porcelain. ⓐ No. 126–128
Perfumes and Cosmetics For leading brands. ⓐ No. 151
Butterfly For audio-visual and photographic equipment. ⓐ No. 152

EXCURSIONS

Ronda
city of the gorge

The old town of Ronda is one of Andalucía's most spectacular and historic towns, famous for its breath-taking scenery, its fine Arab baths and palaces and the oldest bullring in Spain. You will only appreciate its full drama as you enter the town, split in half by a gaping river gorge, the Tajo. The remarkable gorge is spanned by an impressive arched bridge, while tall whitewashed houses lean from its precipitous brink.

Local legend tells that God, fed-up with the constant squabbling of the people of Ronda, sent a huge bolt of lightning down to earth and split the city in two, with the women in one half and the men in the other. This arrangement was so unpopular that they built the bridge across the gorge to reunite the community.

Today, south of the gorge, **La Ciudad** (the old Moorish town) retains its Moorish plan, with many of its fine mansions and the now-Catholic church of Santa María la Mayor, once the town's main mosque. To the north lies El Mercadillo, the new town.

Ronda is the most famous of Andalucía's romantic *pueblos blancos*, the so-called 'white towns' built by the Moors in the 13th century to fend off the harsh rays of the sun. Its stunning location has frequently been used in Hollywood films, including *Carmen* and *For Whom the Bell Tolls*.

> There are some excellent walks around Ronda. One without too much climbing is the footpath called Paseo Blas Infante, which begins behind the *parador* (state-owned hotel housed in a historic building) and leads along the brink of the gorge. An evening stroll along here gives wonderful views. Take your camera.

THINGS TO SEE & DO
La Casa del Rey Moro (Mansion of the Moorish Kings) ★★
This 18th-century mansion overlooking the gorge was built on much older Moorish foundations. Although not open to the public, the house

◆ *Ronda and the impressive El Tajo gorge*

has an ancient underground stairway, which leads right down to the river through terraced gardens. Cut out of the rock by Christian slaves, these 365 steps guaranteed a water supply to the people of the town, even in times of siege. ⓐ Cuesta de Santo Domingo 17 ⓑ Gardens and stairway open 10.00–20.00 (summer); 10.00–19.00 (winter) ⓘ Admission charge

EXCURSIONS

Palacio de Mondragón (Mondragón Palace) ★★★
The palace of the Moorish Kings, built in 1314 by Abomelic, King of Ronda. Much of the original structure remains, notably the coloured patio mosaics and the horseshoe arches. ⓐ Plaza Mondragón ⓣ 952 87 84 50 ⓞ Open Mon–Fri 10.00–19.00, Sat, Sun and hols 10.00–15.00 (summer); 10.00–18.00, Sat, Sun and hols 10.00–15.00 (winter) ⓘ Admission charge

Plaza de Toros (Bullring) ★★
The bullring, built in 1785, is one of the oldest and most beautiful in Spain. It was here that Pedro Romero, the founder of modern bullfighting, evolved today's style of fighting bulls on foot rather than on horseback. Nowadays, the bullring is only used for special fiestas. The museum is well worth a visit. ⓐ Calle Virgen de la Paz 15 ⓣ 952 87 41 32 ⓞ Open 10.00–20.00 ⓘ Admission charge

El Tajo Gorge ★★★
Three bridges span the gorge: the Moorish Puente de San Miguel looks over the ancient Arab baths; the Puente Viejo (Old Bridge) was built in 1616 and the not-so-new Puente Nuevo (New Bridge), built in the late 18th century, boasts unforgettable views and is the symbol of Ronda. The gorge, at its highest point, drops over 90 m (300 ft) to the Guadalevin river below, and has a rather bloody past. The architect of the Puente Nuevo fell to his death here while attempting to catch his hat. In the 18th century, injured horses from the bullring were flung over the cliffs. During the Spanish Civil War, over 500 Nationalist prisoners were thrown into the gorge by Republicans.

RESTAURANTS

Café Alba € A popular breakfast spot, serving delicious coffee, piping hot chocolate and *churros* (akin to a doughnut). ⓐ Calle Espinel 44 ⓣ 952 19 09 53

El Corralillo € This clean, brightly tiled café in a covered passage is a good place to rest your feet while shopping. Good *churros*, breakfasts and snacks. ⓐ Calle Espinel ⓣ 952 87 77 33

RONDA

Don Miguel €€€ The best-placed restaurant in town. The terrace overhangs the gorge and there is a bar actually built into the Puente Nuevo bridge. Expect hearty country fare such as game, partridge stew, and *morcilla rondenos* (Ronda's famous, highly seasoned, black pudding). ⓐ Plaza de España 4 ⓣ 952 87 77 22 ⓦ www.demiguel.com

Doña Pepa €€ Well respected, family-run restaurant offering wholesome *cocido Rondeno* (dishes typical of Ronda), including trout from the mountain streams, rabbit, partridge and quail in garlic. Their separate café-bar opposite serves lighter snacks, *bocadillos* (sandwiches) and freshly squeezed orange juice. ⓐ Plaza del Socorro 10 ⓣ 952 87 47 77

Jerez € Straightforward, authentic local dishes like *migas Ronda-style* (deep-fried breadcrumbs) in a quiet corner behind the bullring. Shady terrace tables in summer. ⓐ Paseo Blas Infante 2 ⓣ 952 87 20 98 ⓦ www.restaurantejerez.com

Pedro Romero €€ Regional specialities served opposite the famous bullring, in a restaurant decorated with a fascinating collection of bull-fighting memorabilia. Try the local favourite, *rabo de toro* (oxtail). ⓐ Virgen de la Paz 18 ⓣ 952 87 11 10 ⓦ www.ronda.net/pedroromero

NIGHTLIFE

Bar Las Castañuelas € A lively local bar where you can enjoy a glass of *fino* (sherry) accompanied by inexpensive, traditional tapas. ⓐ Calle Jerez 3 ⓣ 952 87 61 78

Peña Flamenco Tobalo €€ Some claim that Ronda (and not Sevilla) is the birthplace of flamenco. Live shows take place in Bar la Plazuela most Fridays. Telephone to check. ⓐ Calle Artesanos ⓣ 952 87 41 77 ⓘ Admission charge

EXCURSIONS

White towns
dazzling hilltop sights

Andalucía is full of huddled towns and villages that dazzle on the hilltops. Each consists of a typical Moorish tangle of narrow alleyways lined by whitewashed cottages and flower-filled patios, and many are crowned with castles. Some lie quite close to the coast, and are mentioned elsewhere in this guide (Mijas in the hills behind Fuengirola, Frigiliana near Nerja, or Mojácar on the Costa de Almería).

Many of the best-known white villages lie near Ronda. Organized excursions visit a few of them from the coastal resorts, but if you have your own transport you can choose your own picnic route through some splendid rugged scenery (it is unlikely you would be able to cover all the villages in one day). Pick up a tourist office leaflet for some itinerary ideas.

WHITE TOWNS

◀ Casares, *pueblo blanco*

- **Arcos de la Frontera** Reaching this sizeable town involves a hair-raising climb through the old quarter. A *parador* and a fine Gothic church teeter on the edge of a spectacular cliff where hawks practise hang-gliding.
- **Benaoján** Famed for its caves. The Cueva de la Pileta contains prehistoric wall-paintings.
- **Casares** White houses spill down a steep hillside.
- **Gaucín** The ridge-top setting with marvellous views attracts many visitors – some set up home here.
- **Grazalema** One of the prettiest of all the *pueblos*. The tourist office probably won't tell you that it has the highest rainfall in Spain (hence its surprisingly lush surroundings).
- **Jimena de la Frontera** A ruined Moorish castle dominates a landscape of cork oaks, olives and fighting bulls.
- **Medina Sidonia** An aristocratic town of imposing palaces.
- **Olvera** A dramatic landslide of glittering houses below a castle.
- **Setenil** A river-gorge of volcanic tufa adds an unusual setting to Setenil's white houses; some have roofs of natural rock.
- **Ubrique** A thriving leather industry keeps souvenir-hunters happy in this bustling town.
- **Vejer de la Frontera** It's a long drive to this little place near Cape Trafalgar, but Vejer is one of the most memorable and traditional of these African-looking settlements.
- **Zahara de la Sierra** Now declared a national monument, this striking village of red-tiled houses on an arid castle-crowned rock will keep your camera snapping.

On the journey from the coast into the rugged Serranía de Ronda mountains, watch out for mountain hare, deer, wild partridge and the endangered Spanish ibex (wild goat), while golden eagles, lesser kestrels and griffon vultures wheel in the sky.

EXCURSIONS

Mijas
a photographer's dream

Just 8 km (5 miles) inland from the modern urban sprawl of Fuengirola, set amongst tranquil pine groves on the edge of the Sierra de Mijas mountains, this quaint, picture-postcard *pueblo blanco* (white village) is a photographer's dream. This is Andalucía at its picturesque best, with its hilly, cobbled streets, wrought-iron balconies cascading with flowers, donkey taxis, unique square bullring and breathtaking coastal views.

Like most of the villages situated in this region, Mijas (which is pronounced '*me*-hass') has Roman, Phoenician and Moorish origins. Its present layout dates back to Moorish times, when the village served as a granary for Fuengirola and a defence against the Christians. In the 17th and 18th centuries, Mijas housed the workers of the now-disused marble quarries in the hills. The marble cut from these quarries was used to build the cathedral in Málaga and the Alcazaba in Córdoba. It then became a farming community until the tourism boom of the 1960s and 1970s.

At first Mijas was a must-see for every visitor then, after a while, many of the foreign visitors decided it was a great place to live and began to build property on the gentle slopes of the Sierra between Mijas and the coast. Today, expat residents outnumber Spaniards and the views from the village towards the Mediterranean are dotted with their luxury villas, sparkling azure swimming pools and golf courses rather than avocado-pear plantations.

The village is still very much a tourist attraction, thriving on its local handicrafts of ceramics, leather and lace. Its dazzling white streets are filled with bars and restaurants. Horse-drawn carriages or *burro taxis* (donkey taxis) carry visitors away from the crowded centre, up the steep, narrow parts, where Mijas has conserved its rustic charm and sleepy Andalucían atmosphere.

▶ *Mijas' streets have a rustic charm*

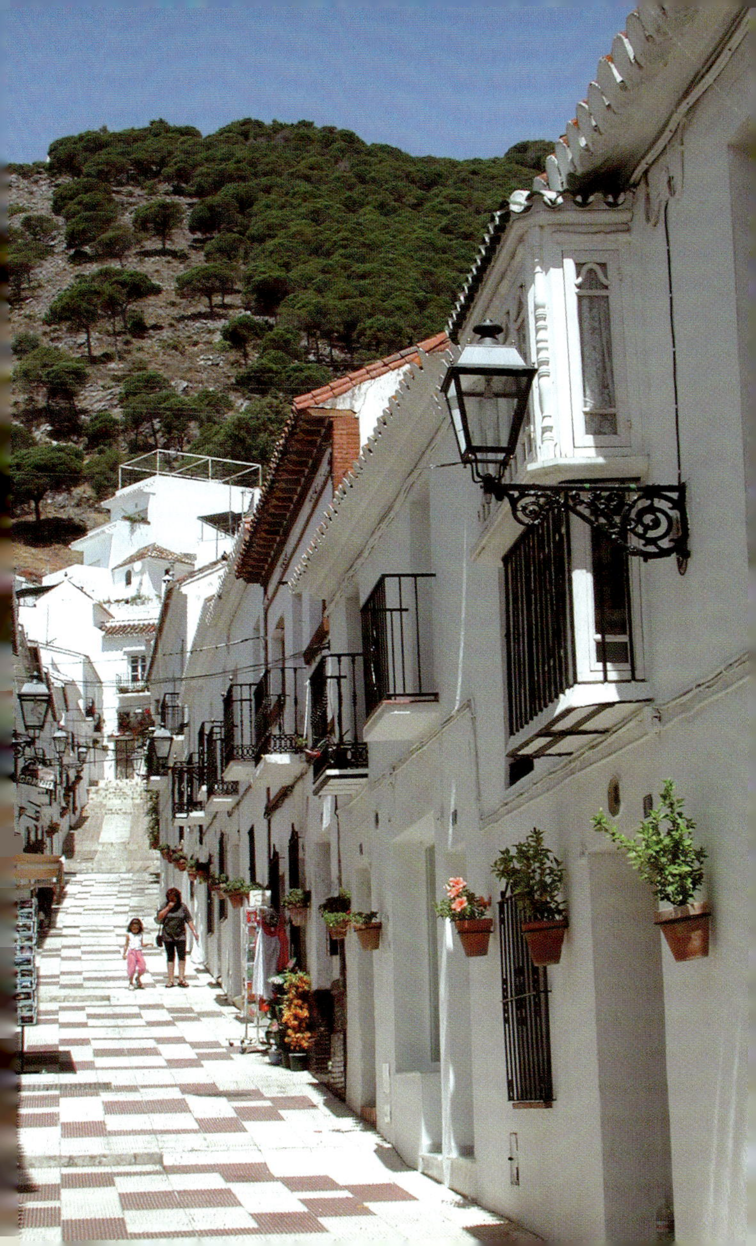

EXCURSIONS

> The best time to visit Mijas is just before sunset when most tourists have retreated to the coast; the shops are still open and the light is at its best for photographs.

THINGS TO SEE & DO

Carromato de Max (Museum of Miniatures) ★
This must be the most peculiar museum on the entire coast, with such exhibits (all under magnifying glasses) as the 'seven wonders of the world' painted on a toothpick and a bullfight painted on a lentil, not to mention a dressed flea. ⓐ Avenida del Compás ⓛ Open 10.00–22.00 ⓘ Admission charge

Ermita del Calvario (Chapel of Calvary) ★★
For the best views in town, climb up to the tiny chapel of the Calvary high above the village. The walk, through cool pine groves, following a trail of black iron crosses, takes about 30 minutes. At the top, you will be well rewarded with breathtaking views from Gibraltar to Africa.

Golf ★★
Mijas is famous for its top-quality golf courses, drawing thousands of enthusiasts every year. Los Lagos and Los Olivos are popular courses near Mijas, as is **Mijas-Golf** ⓐ Carretera Coín, Km 3 ⓣ 952 47 68 43 ⓦ www.mijasgolf.com ⓛ Open daily

Tennis ★★
Mijas's tennis club, founded by the late Lew Hoad, has courts to rent, special coaching programmes and mini tournaments. **Campo de Tenis Lew Hoad** ⓐ Carretera de Mijas, Km 3.5 ⓣ 952 47 48 58 ⓦ www.tennis-spain.com ⓛ Open to public, Tues and Thurs, all year round

RESTAURANTS & BARS

La Alcazaba €€€ Beautiful Moorish-looking restaurant commanding wonderful views from a prime clifftop location. ⓐ Alcazaba, Plaza de la Constitución ⓣ 952 59 02 53 ⓛ Open Tues–Sun

SHOPPING

Amapola Offers tiny pots, jewellery and other trinkets decorated with dried wild flowers from the countryside.
ⓐ Alcazaba, Plaza de la Constitucion ⓣ 952 48 62 54

Artesanía de España Probably the best choice of pottery in town.
ⓐ Calle Málaga 2 ⓣ 952 48 62 03

Artesanía Rocío A tiny, old-fashioned shop selling Spanish lace.
ⓐ Pasaje Salvador Cantón Jimenez ⓣ 610 03 68 18 (mobile)

Guantería Costa del Sol Leather bags, belts, wallets ... and how about an extra suitcase for all your presents and souvenirs?
ⓐ Calle Los Caños 17 ⓣ 952 48 59 46

El Shop Try here for timeless yet useful gift ideas such as candlesticks, picture frames, hand-cast in brass and aluminium.
ⓐ Alcazaba, Plaza de la Constitucion ⓣ 952 59 03 07

Tamisa Lladró porcelain, Mallorcan pearls and beautiful traditionally styled jewellery of filigree silver, brass and copper – a speciality of Mijas. ⓐ Alcazaba, Plaza de la Constitución ⓣ 952 48 51 41
ⓦ www.tamisashop.com

Bar Porras € This friendly, no-frills bar provides a good opportunity to meet the locals over a beer and a plate of tapas.
ⓐ Plaza Libertad 3 ⓣ 952 48 50 41

El Mirlo Blanco €€ 'The White Blackbird' is a thoroughly Spanish, family-run restaurant near the bullring. Whatever you order don't miss the unusual puddings, such as *leche frita* (thick custard cut into squares then fried). Delicious! ⓐ Plaza de la Constitucion 2
ⓣ 952 48 57 00

El Olivar €€ Typical Andalucían interior and good views. Spanish tapas. ⓐ Avenida Virgen de la Peña ⓣ 952 48 61 96
ⓒ Closed Sat and Feb

Córdoba Map

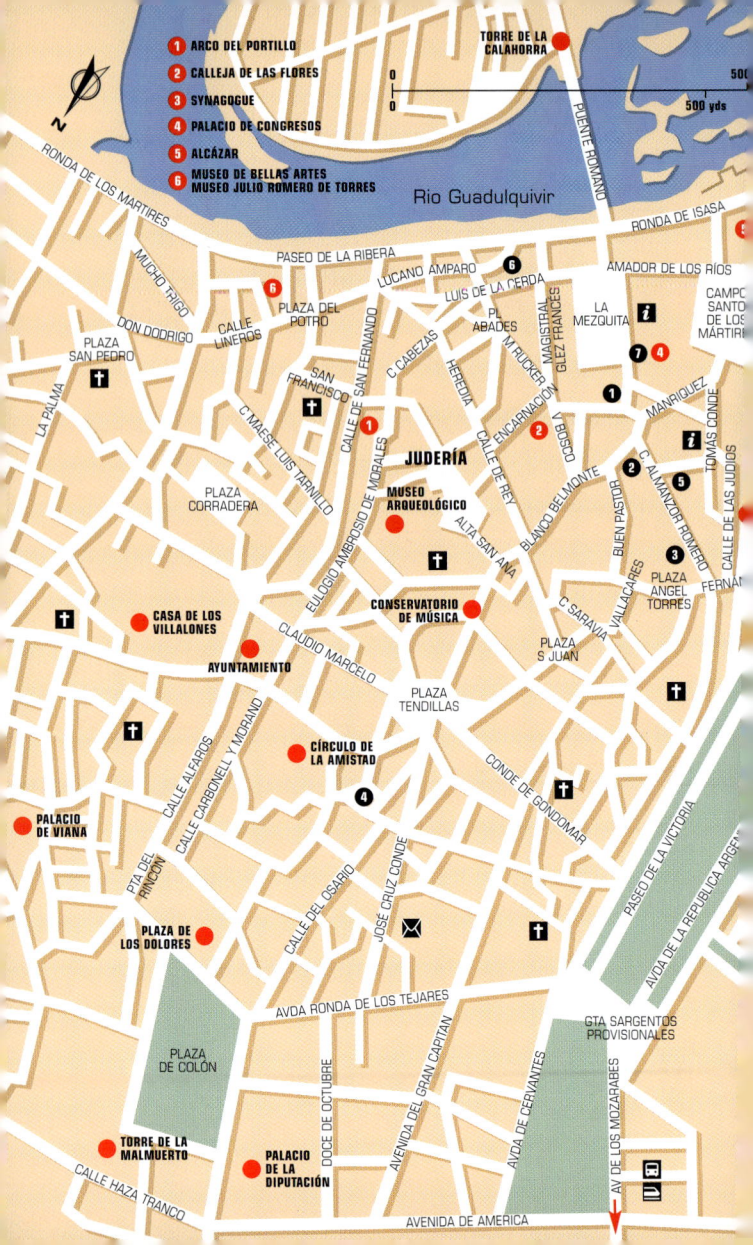

Legend
1. ARCO DEL PORTILLO
2. CALLEJA DE LAS FLORES
3. SYNAGOGUE
4. PALACIO DE CONGRESOS
5. ALCÁZAR
6. MUSEO DE BELLAS ARTES / MUSEO JULIO ROMERO DE TORRES

Points of Interest
- TORRE DE LA CALAHORRA
- PUENTE ROMANO
- Rio Guadulquivir
- LA MEZQUITA
- CAMPO SANTO DE LOS MÁRTIRES
- JUDERÍA
- MUSEO ARQUEOLÓGICO
- CONSERVATORIO DE MÚSICA
- CASA DE LOS VILLALONES
- AYUNTAMIENTO
- PLAZA TENDILLAS
- CÍRCULO DE LA AMISTAD
- PALACIO DE VIANA
- PLAZA DE LOS DOLORES
- PLAZA DE COLÓN
- TORRE DE LA MALMUERTO
- PALACIO DE LA DIPUTACIÓN

Plazas
- PLAZA SAN PEDRO
- PLAZA DEL POTRO
- PLAZA CORRADERA
- PLAZA ANGEL TORRES
- PLAZA S JUAN

Streets
- RONDA DE LOS MARTIRES
- RONDA DE ISASA
- PASEO DE LA RIBERA
- LUCANO AMPARO
- LUIS DE LA CERDA
- AMADOR DE LOS RÍOS
- MUCHO TRIGO
- DON DRODIGO
- CALLE LINEROS
- M RUCKER
- MAGISTRAL GLEZ FRANCES
- LA PALMA
- C CABEZAS
- HEREDIA
- ENCARNACIÓN
- V BOSCO
- MANRIQUEZ
- CALLE DE SAN FERNANDO
- SAN FRANCISCO
- C/MAESE LUIS TARRILLO
- CALLE DE REY
- BLANCO BELMONTE
- C ALMANZOR ROMERO
- TOMÁS CONDE
- CALLE DE LOS JUDIOS
- EULOGIO AMBROSIO DE MORALES
- ALTA SAN ANA
- BUEN PASTOR
- VALLCARES
- C SARAVIA
- FERNÁN
- CLAUDIO MARCELO
- CALLE ALFAROS
- CALLE CARBONELL Y MORAND
- PTA DEL RINCÓN
- CONDE DE GONDOMAR
- PASEO DE LA VICTORIA
- AVDA DE LA REPÚBLICA ARGE
- CALLE DEL OSARIO
- JOSÉ CRUZ CONDE
- AVDA RONDA DE LOS TEJARES
- DOCE DE OCTUBRE
- AVENIDA DEL GRAN CAPITAN
- AVDA DE CERVANTES
- AV DE LOS MOZARABES
- CALLE HAZA TRANCO
- AVENIDA DE AMERICA
- GTA SARGENTOS PROVISIONALES

Córdoba
Moorish masterpiece

Situated in the fertile valley of the Guadalquivir river, the ancient city of Córdoba remains comparatively untouched by tourism and is one of Andalucía's most precious jewels, a city of churches, mansions, museums and La Mezquita – a masterpiece of Islamic art and one of the largest mosques in the world.

THINGS TO SEE & DO
Judería (Jewish Quarter) ★★★
This is the prettiest district of Córdoba – a charming tangle of narrow whitewashed streets and alleys, with brilliantly coloured flowers spilling over from every balcony. Wooden doors open onto some of the loveliest patios in Andalucía, adorned with fountains and blue ceramic tiles and shaded by palm and orange trees. One of the most picturesque streets is Calleja de las Flores. By day, you can also find some delightful souvenirs in its many small shops, and by night people flock to its restaurants and bars to sing flamenco and dance *sevillanas*.

La Mezquita (The Great Mosque) ★★★
This is the most important Islamic monument in the western world and no guidebook can adequately prepare you for its grandeur; you enter through a patio of orange trees into the ancient, dimly lit mosque – a forest of stone columns and double red and cream arches. For the most spectacular view of the city and the mountains beyond, climb what seems like thousands of steps to the top of La Mezquita's Minaret Tower. Your efforts will be well rewarded! ❸ Calle Cardenal Herrero 1 ❶ 957 47 05 12 ❷ Open daily. Last entry 30 mins before closing. Evening opening varies each month. Excellent access for visitors with disabilities ❶ Admission charge

Palacio de Viana (Viana Palace) ★★

This lovely 16th-century palace is the former seat of the Marquises of Viana. Its best feature is its 'Museum of Courtyards' – a dozen flower-filled patios, each one differently designed. They reach their peak of perfection in May, in time for the Fiesta de los Patios. ⓐ Plaza Don Gome 2 ⓘ 957 49 67 41 ⓛ Open Mon–Sat 09.00–14.00 (summer); Mon–Fri 10.00–13.00 and 16.00–18.00, Sat 10.00–13.00 (winter), closed 1–15 June ⓘ Admission charge

Plaza del Potro ★★

Don't miss this atmospheric old cobbled square, named after the lively *potro* (colt) rearing above its fountain. Posada del Potro, a quaint old inn where Cervantes stayed, now houses the Casa de Cultura. Also here is the **Museo de Bellas Artes (Fine Arts Museum)**, containing orthodox works by a number of Spanish masters. ⓘ 957 47 33 45 ⓛ Open Tues, Wed–Sat 09.00–20.30 ⓘ Admission free with EU passport. Next to this is the rather more *louche* **Museo Julio Romero de Torres**, dedicated to a local artist (1885–1930) whose kitschy female nudes continue to arouse much controversy. ⓘ 957 49 19 09 ⓛ Open Tues–Sat ⓘ Admission charge, but free on Fri with EU passport

RESTAURANTS (see map on page 76)

El Caballo Rojo €€€ ❶ For a special occasion, this classic restaurant by the Mezquita is famous for its Andalucían dishes with an Arab influence. ⓐ Calle Cardenal Herrero 28 ⓘ 957 47 53 75 ⓦ www.elcaballorojo.com ⓘ No wheelchair access

---

SHOPPING

The main shops are along **Calle Conde de Gondomar** and **Calle Claudio Marcelo** on either side of **Plaza Tendillas**. There is also a clothes and crafts market every morning in **Plaza de la Corredera**.

La Mezquita

Casa Pepe €€ ❷ One of Córdoba's best-loved restaurants. Try the *salmorejo* (salt of the Moors), a soup unique to Córdoba (like *gazpacho* but with ham and egg). Calle A Romero 1 • 957 20 07 44

El Churrasco €€ ❸ This small, intimate restaurant is an old favourite in Córdoba. It specializes in grilled meats, served at tables on an attractive patio. Calle A Romero 16 • 957 29 08 19 • www.elchurrasco.com

Il Pisto (aka Taberna San Miguel) € ❹ Come here for a wide choice of good-value tapas dishes. The spicy *chorizo* (Spanish sausage) and *patatas ailioli* (potatoes with garlic mayonnaise) are especially delicious. Plaza San Miguel 1 • 957 47 83 28

El Rincón de Carmen €€ ❺ A charming open-air courtyard is a good start, but the friendly service, generous portions and good cooking promise an enjoyable meal. Calle A Romero 4 • 957 29 10 55

El Tablón € ❻ Close to the Mezquita, offering good-value set menus and *platos combinados* in a pretty Andaluz courtyard dining room. Cardenal González 69 • 957 47 60 61

NIGHTLIFE
Tablao Cardenal ❼ The best open-air flamenco show in town.
Calle Torrijos 10 (next door to the tourist office) • 957 48 33 20
• Performances at 22.30 (except Sun) • Reserve a table in advance

EXCURSIONS

Málaga
capital of the Costa del Sol

Málaga is a bustling seaport, the sprawling capital of the Costa, the second city of Andalucía and the sixth biggest city in Spain. You either love it or you hate it, but there is no denying, it is one of the most Spanish of cities – atmospheric and vibrant. What's more, the inhabitants are among the friendliest people in Spain.

THINGS TO SEE & DO
La Alcazaba (Moorish Fortress) ★★
The remains of an 11th-century Moorish fortress stand in attractive fountain-splashed gardens high above the city. Its terraces afford photogenic vistas of Málaga and its glittering bay. ⓐ Calle Alcazabilla ⓘ 952 21 60 05 ⓒ Open Tues–Sun 09.30–20.00 (summer); 09.30–19.00 (winter) ⓘ Admission charge

Antequera ★★
The town of Antequera is easily reached by car or public transport from Málaga. It's usually a quiet town, but it livens up on Fridays when its market is in full swing. Most of its monuments are shut on Mondays. The old centre contains an impressive list of monuments, including several large churches (Nuestra Señora del Carmen, Santa María, San Agustín and San Sebastián), a ruined Arab fortress (Alcazaba) and an archway (Arco de los Gigantes) dating from the 16th century. Both the

> ### SHOPPING
> The three main streets – **Calle Marqués de Larios, Calle Molina Lario** and **Calle de Granada** – are all lined with shops and fashion boutiques, while the tastes, fragrances and colours of the Mediterranean at **Mercado Atarazanas**, the daily provisions market, are a veritable feast for the senses.

town hall (Palacio Consistorial) and the museum (Museo Municipal) occupy fine palaces. Antequera's most unusual sights, though, are its dolmen caves, easily found on the approach road from Málaga. These megalithic monuments are believed to be around 4500 years old.

Castillo de Gibralfaro (Gibralfaro Castle) ★★
One of Málaga's great landmarks, this Moorish castle perched high above the city was built sometime in the early 14th century on the site of an ancient lighthouse. At the foot of the Castillo is a Roman ampitheatre. ⓐ Monte de Gibralfaro ⓛ Open 09.30–20.00 ⓘ Joint ticket with La Alcazaba

Cathedral ★★
Málaga's cathedral took over 350 years to build. The original plans included two towers but the money ran out, so only one was completed, giving rise to the affectionate nickname, La Manquita ('the little one-armed woman'). ⓐ Calle Molina Lario ⓣ 952 22 84 91 ⓛ Open Mon–Fri 10.00–18.45, Sat 10.00–17.30, closed for sightseeing on Sun
ⓘ Admission charge

Competa ★★
Explore the Axarquia's inland villages. You can follow the Ruta del Vino (wine route) 22 km (13.75 miles) from the coast, stopping at the villages that produce the sweet local wine, particularly Competa. Alternatively, take the Ruta de la Pasa (raisin route) through Moclinejo, El Borge and Comares; the latter has an incredible position, perched atop one of the highest mountains, and dates back to Moorish times.

El Chorro ★★
North of Málaga the River Guadalhorce cuts a dramatic gorge through sheer 30 m (100 ft) cliffs that make irresistible targets for rock-climbers. Above the gorge are the reservoir lakes which supply most of Málaga's water. The scenery in this craggy area is spectacular, and offers many opportunities for walks and picnics.

EXCURSIONS

La Concepción ★★
This marvellous tropical garden on the city's outskirts has been growing for a century and half. An Englishwoman married to the Marquis of Casa Loring assembled this collection of rare and exotic plants, one of Spain's most important gardens. ⓐ Carretera de las Pedrizas, Km 166 (off the Antequera road) ⓣ 952 25 21 48 ⓦ www.manilvalife.com ⓞ Open Tues–Sun 10.00–19.30 ⓘ Visits by guided tour only

Picasso Museums ★★
The artist Pablo Picasso was born in Málaga in 1881. His birthplace, the **Casa Natal de Picasso**, contains an exhibition of photographs of Picasso as a child, plus memorabilia and early works. ⓐ Plaza de la Merced ⓣ 952 06 02 15 ⓞ Open Mon–Sat 10.00–14.00 and 17.00–20.00, Sun 11.00– 14.00) ⓘ Admission free

In a nearby street, part of the former Museo de Bellas Artes, a 16th-century palace, has been restored to house a **Picasso Museum**, containing around 140 major works. ⓐ Calle San Agustin 8 ⓦ www.museopicassomalaga.org ⓘ Admission charge

El Torcal ★★
South of Antequera lies a weird wonderland of eroded limestone outcrops which in places look like stacks of dinner plates. Rare plants and birds of prey colonize the region, which is one of Andalucía's most spectacular natural parks. The strange formations are best seen towards sundown, when the shadows are sharpest. El Torcal features regularly on excursion programmes from the coastal resorts. For more information, contact the park information centre: **Centro de Visitantes**. ⓣ 952 03 13 89 ⓞ Open 10.00–14.00, 15.00–17.00 (Nov–May); 10.00–14.00, 16.00–18.00 (June–Oct)

RESTAURANTS & BARS
Málaga is famed for its old *bodegas* (wine bars) and tapas bars, which provide a good opportunity to try local delicacies and the sweet local wine, while the smart seafront promenade boasts some of the best fish restaurants in the province.

MÁLAGA

The bustling seaport of Málaga

Antigua Casa del Guardia € The oldest *bodega* in town, lined with barrels and an excellent place to sample some of Málaga's sweet wines. ⓐ Calle Alameda Principal 18 ⓣ 952 21 46 80

Antonio Martín €€€ A popular seafront restaurant specializing in seafood. ⓐ Paseo Marítimo ⓣ 952 22 73 82

El Chinitas €€ This is a great favourite with Malagans for tapas, especially the delicious Andalucian dishes. ⓐ Calle Moreno Monroy 4–6 ⓣ 952 21 09 72 ⓦ www.chinitas.arrakis.es

EXCURSIONS

Granada
Moorish heritage

If you only visit one city during your stay in Spain, it should be Granada, a historic city just two hours' drive from Málaga – set against a backdrop of snow-capped mountains of the Sierra Nevada – and home to the exquisite Alhambra Palace, often described as the eighth wonder of the world.

> The best photo opportunity in Granada is late afternoon at the Mirador de San Nicolás – the highest point in the Albaicín quarter – for stunning shots of the Alhambra glowing red in the evening sun.

THINGS TO SEE & DO
Albaicín (Ancient Arab Quarter) ★★
The Arab quarter's picturesque, cobbled streets of whitewashed houses cling to the hillside facing the Alhambra, punctuated by tiny fountain-filled squares and hidden patios of lemon trees, pomegranates and vines. Beyond the hill, a few of Granada's gypsy population still live in the Sacromonte cave dwellings. Some of the caves, such as Los Faroles, now stage flamenco spectacles, and the ones above Casa del Chapiz are popular weekend disco haunts during university term-time.

Alhambra and Generalife ★★★
The Alhambra is one of the world's most remarkable, harmonious collections of 14th-century Arabic palaces, fortifications, domes and ornamental gardens, which represent the epitome of Moorish architecture with their mosaics, marble balustrades, carved wooden ceilings and fine filigree stonework. The pink-tinged walls explain the name (*al-hamra* means 'the red'). There are three distinct groups of buildings on Alhambra Hill: the Casa Real or Royal Palace – the real gem of the Alhambra, the Generalife gardens, and the oldest section, the Alcazaba, dating from the 10th to 13th centuries. ❶ 958 22 09 12 ❿ www.alhambra-patronato.es ❶ Open daily, with seasonal variations ❶ Admission charge

Granada Map

Labeled locations:

- CARMEN DE LOS MÁRTIRES
- CENTRO CULTURAL MANUEL DE FALLA
- MUSEO
- NUESTRA SEÑORA DE LAS ANGUSTIAS
- EL GENERALIFE
- ALHAMBRA
- IGLESIA DE SANTA DOMINGO
- PLAZA BIBATAUBÍN
- PLAZA DEL CAMPILLO
- PLAZA DEL CARMEN
- CORRAL DEL CARBÓN
- ALCAICERÍA
- PLAZA BIB-RAMBLA
- CASA DE CASTRIL
- EL BAÑUELO
- MUSEO SAN JUAN DE DIOS
- PLAZA STA. ANA
- PLAZA NUEVA
- PALACIO DE LA MADRAZA
- CAPILLA REAL
- PLAZA TRINIDAD
- ALBAICÍN
- MONASTERIO DE SANTA ISABEL LA REAL
- PLAZA LOBOS
- IGLESIA DE SAN JERÓNIMO
- MURALLAS DEL ALBAICÍN
- PARQUE DE LAS CIENCIAS
- SIERRA NEVADA

Streets (selected):

- PASEO DE LOS BASILIOS
- PASEO DE LA BOMBA
- PASEO DEL SALÓN
- MANUEL DE GÓNGORA
- CUESTA DE CALDERO
- PASEO DE LOS MÁRTIRES
- ANTEQUERUELA BAJA
- BELÉN
- CALLE DE MOLINOS
- CALLE DE SANTIAGO
- PACO SECO DE LUCENA
- CABRERA DEL GERILL
- CONCEPCIÓN
- ACERA DEL DARRO
- CAMPO DEL PRÍNCIPE
- AIRE ALTA
- CALLE NIÑO DEL ROYO
- CRUZ DE PIEDRA
- PL S DOMINGO
- CALLE SAN MATÍAS
- ACERA DEL CASINO
- CUESTA DEL REY CHICO
- PASEO DEL PADRE MANJÓN
- ZACATÍN
- MESONES
- CUESTA DEL CHAPIZ
- ZAIRA
- CALDERERÍA NUEVA
- CJON MARÍA DE LA MIEL
- CJON NEVOT
- CUESTA DE LA BETETA
- CALLE DE ELVIRA
- GRAN VÍA DE COLÓN
- SAN JERÓNIMO
- SANTA PAULA
- CJON S CECILIO
- CTA MARÍA DE LA MIEL
- CRUZ DE QUIRÓS
- ZENETE
- ARANDOS
- SAN LUIS
- S BUENAVENTURA
- CUESTA ALBAHACA
- CARRIL DE LA LONA
- PERNALEGRO ALTO
- ACERA DE S LOPERENZA
- GRAN CAPITÁN
- RECTOR LÓPEZ ARGUETA
- DE PIEDRA
- CAMINO DE SAN ANTONIO

VISITING THE SIGHTS

A maximum of 8800 visitors are allowed into the Alhambra each day, so you should reserve in advance via any branch of the BBV bank, including the one on Plaza Isabel la Católica (a small commission is charged; ask the tourist office for details). Timed combined tickets are issued for the Alhambra's various sections: the Palacios Nazaries (royal palace), the Generalife gardens and the Alcazaba fortress.

You must enter the palace complex within your allocated half-hour slot, but you can stay as long as you like. If you have to wait, you can visit the Alcazaba at any time, or while away an hour or so in the pleasant cafés and restaurants nearby.

To save the hassle of driving and expensive car-parking, take the Alhambra minibus (marked Conexión Alhambra–Albayzín (Albaicín), every ten minutes from Plaza Nueva). This useful service also saves the steep climb to the Albaicín, stopping near the San Nicolás mirador.

Capilla Real *(Royal Chapel)* ★★

The impressive Royal Chapel adjoining the vast Gothic cathedral, contains the tombs of the Catholic monarchs, Ferdinand and Isabella, who were the conquerors of Granada. ⓐ Calle Oficios ⓣ 958 22 92 39 ⓦ www.capillarealgranada.com ⓞ Open Mon–Sat 10.30–13.00 and 16.00–19.00, Sun 11.00–13.00 (and Sun 16.00–19.00 in summer)

Parque de las Ciencias (Science Museum) ★

This fascinating science museum which incorporates a planetarium should appeal to visitors of all ages with its interesting range of hands-on multi-media displays and experiments. ⓐ Avenida del Mediterráneo ⓣ 958 13 19 00 ⓦ www.parqueciencia.com
ⓞ Open Tues–Sat 10.00–19.00, Sun 10.00–15.00
ⓘ Admission charge

GRANADA

RESTAURANTS (see map on pages 85)

El Agua €€ ❶ Fondue restaurant with fantastic views of the palace. ⓐ Plaza Aljibe de Trillo 7 ❶ 958 22 33 58
🕒 Open Wed–Mon 13.30–15.30 and 16.00–23.30, Tues 16.00–23.00

Alhambra Palace Hotel €€€ ❷ Come here for an early evening drink to enjoy the brilliant views of the city from the terrace at sunset. ⓐ Calle Peña Partida 2–4 ❶ 958 22 14 68

Cunini €€€ ❸ A long-established traditional favourite in the city centre, specializing in excellent seafood. Tapas are served at the bar, but book ahead for a table. ⓐ Plaza Pescadería 14 ❶ 958 25 07 77
🕒 Closed Mon and Sun eve

Granero de Abrantes €€€ ❹ This stylish place with a high-raftered ceiling has a sophisticated menu (cod with raisins and pine kernels or Alpujarras asparagus soup). Excellent bread. ⓐ Plaza Poeta Luis Rosales, just off the main square ❶ 958 50 80 64

Mirador de Morayma €€€ ❺ A charming way to enjoy views of the Alhambra, from the shady gardens of a 16th-century Albaicín house. ⓐ Calle Pianista García Carrillo 2 ❶ 958 22 82 90
🕒 Open Mon–Sat; Flamenco show Tues 23.00

Parador €€ ❻ The terrace café of Granada's elegant state-owned hotel is less expensive than its formal restaurant, overlooking the Generalife Gardens. ⓐ Real de la Alhambra
❶ 958 22 14 40 Ⓦ www.parador.es

Sevilla €€ ❼ Steeped in history, this popular restaurant/tapas bar was the preferred haunt of local writer, García Lorca, and of composer, Manuel de Falla. The 1930s dining room remains unchanged.
ⓐ Calle Oficios 12 ❶ 958 22 12 23 Ⓦ www.alqueriamorayma.com
🕒 Closed Sun eve

EXCURSIONS

Mojácar
trendsetting *pueblo*

A dazzling pile of cube-shaped houses scattered on a rocky hilltop, a long beach dotted with palms and spiky agaves cactus – the picture conjured by this *pueblo blanca* in the remotest and most arid part of south-eastern Spain spells Andalucía in bold letters. In a way, though, the village is an artificial community, recreated by outsiders who 'rediscovered' it during the 1960s and appreciated its distinctive character.

Many of its former inhabitants, debilitated by the Spanish Civil War, had emigrated in search of work and its pretty houses had slid into ruin. An enterprising local mayor encouraged new settlers by offering free plots of building land, and a cosmopolitan colony of artists flocked here in search of an alternative lifestyle. Today, Mojácar is a chic and successful holiday resort that has retained its charm despite inevitable expansion to cater for its new visitors. The water is exceptionally clear, and a good range of watersports is available, including diving and fishing. The region is well worth exploring; there are a number of unusual sights and some spectacular scenery nearby. Excursions are organized from the village, but to see the area conveniently, car hire is recommended.

THINGS TO SEE & DO
Boat trips ★★
Take a relaxing mini cruise along the rugged, unspoilt coast.
Daily excursion boats ❷ From Garrucha (a short distance to the north) to the Cabo de Gata; ferry Costa de Níjar, Puerto Deportivo de Garrucha ❶ 950 46 00 48
Fishing or dolphin-spotting trips ❷ Advertised near the beach, Lolailo Lailo II ❶ 639 21 75 05

Mojácar Pueblo ★★★
Most hotels and apartments are down near the beach, but whatever you do, don't miss a chance to explore the old hilltop village 2 km (1 mile)

● *Mojácar is a distinctive sight on a rocky hilltop*

inland. There are no particular sights, but it is one of Andalucía's most charming 'white towns', full of fascinating little shops and restaurants. The views from its *miradors* are spectacular. Most of its activity centres around the main squares of Plaza Nueva, Plaza de la Iglesia and Plaza del Ayuntamiento.

Parque Acuático Vera ★

The local answer to all those Costa del Sol water parks. This one lies near Vera, a little way north of Mojácar. ❸ Carretera Vera/Garrucha–Villaricos ❶ 950 46 73 37 Ⓦ www.aquavera.com ❶ Open daily, with seasonal variations

EXCURSIONS

RESTAURANTS
Mojácar Beach
The long seafront road has plenty of apartments, shops and eating places, and they are much less oppressive than in many resorts, in simple local styles.

Antonela €€ This is an elegant Italian establishment with very good terrace views over the sea. ⓐ Paseo del Mediterráneo ⓣ 950 47 22 24 ⓛ Dinner only

La Cantina €€ A delightful Mexican-style complex of beachside bar and bistro – nachos and tacos galore. The location is exceptionally good, right by the beach in a shady patch of palms. ⓐ Playa Las Ventanicas ⓣ 950 47 88 41 ⓦ www.lacantinamojacar.com ⓛ Closed Mon off-season; beach bar closed in winter; dinner only

India Tandoori € Just what it says, offering straightforward, well-cooked curries at good prices. ⓐ Paseo del Mediterráneo ⓣ 950 47 21 14 ⓛ Dinner only

Restaurante El Viento del Desierto € Very reasonable starters and main courses of the local game. Situated just beside the church. ⓐ Plaza Frontón ⓣ 950 47 86 26 ⓛ Open 20.00–23.00

San Bernabe €€€ This restaurant offers a smarter ambience than most along the seafront, but it also has a welcoming atmosphere. Attractive menu and elegant terrace dining. ⓐ Playa, attached to the Hotel Felipe ⓣ 950 47 82 02 ⓔ sanbernabe@interbook.net ⓦ www.mojacaronline.com ⓛ Open Fri–Wed

Mojácar Town
Heladería Amalia € A very civilized ice cream spot situated on a quiet pretty square below the church. ⓐ Plaza del Parterre ⓛ Open in summer only

MOJÁCAR

> **THE INDALO**
> Everywhere around Mojácar you will see a stick-like figure with an arc above its head. This is the Indalo, a symbol found in neolithic cave drawings at nearby **Vélez Blanco**. For centuries, this matchstick man was painted on the doors of local houses to ward off evil and bring good luck to the inhabitants. It is now used as the Costa de Almería's publicity logo.

Mamabel's €€ A delightful little hotel-restaurant overlooking splendid views. Typical Andalucían-style decor. A shortish but interesting menu, and flamenco on Saturdays. ⓐ Calle Embajadores 5 ⓣ 950 47 24 48 ⓦ www.mamabels.com ⓞ Open for breakfast and dinner

Palacio €€ A smart little place in the village centre offering interesting dishes like fresh salmon in prune sauce or leek cake. ⓐ Plaza del Caño ⓣ 950 47 28 46 ⓞ Dinner only

NIGHTLIFE

A number of open-air discos cater for the small hours on the beach, but many are seasonal and may open only at weekends except in high summer.

Badgers Aston Villa fans should make a pilgrimage here. Keith Bradley (an ex-player) runs this lively seafront bar. Plenty of televised football, karaoke and traditional British cooking. ⓐ Paseo del Mediterráneo ⓣ 950 47 85 25

Bora Bora A lively bar, with DJs, quiz nights and beach parties. ⓐ Right on the beach ⓣ 687 66 38 80 ⓞ Open until 03.00

Pascha One of the biggest and most popular discos. ⓐ On the seafront near Camping El Cantal. Paseo del Mediterráneo

EXCURSIONS

Almería
fortress town

The provincial capital is a town with a very distinguished past, though not much of its former glory survives today. Its Alcazaba, dating from AD 995, was the largest fortress ever built by the Moors in Spain, which gives some idea of what an important place it was. Under the Caliphate of Córdoba, it was a major port for the export of textiles, particularly the silk produced in vast quantities in Las Alpujarras. Gradually, sieges and economic decline took their toll. Today Almería is a dusty little city, extremely poor in places. Its main landmarks, though, are worth a brief visit, and it has some atmospheric, inexpensive tapas bars and nightlife.

THINGS TO SEE & DO

Mojácar (see page 88) could be combined with any of these excursions, or used as a starting point.

Alcazaba (Moorish Castle) ★★★

An impressive example of Moorish fortification, this massive castle was badly damaged in an earthquake in 1522. The three separate wards of the fortress and many of the walls are still intact, however, and offer a splendid vantage point over the town and port. ⓐ Calle Almanzor
ⓘ 950 27 16 17 ⓛ Open Tues–Sun 09.00–16.30 (June–Sept); 09.30–18.30 (Oct–July) ⓘ Free with EU passport

---

The old fishing and gypsy quarter of La Chanca near the Alcazaba is a picturesque if raffish area of brightly painted, cube-shaped houses, some built into caves in the rocks. Take care if you want to explore it. Holidaymakers are prime targets for thieves. It is unwise to carry cameras and valuables, or to go alone at night.

Cabo de Gata ★★

On the east side of town stretches the hilly cape which marks Spain's south-eastern tip. There's a fine sandy beach here (mainly used by locals), but very little natural shade. This is one of the driest and hottest regions of Spain, and summer temperatures are ferocious. Much of it is a natural park of briny lagoons similar to the ones near Almerimar. Piles of salt are extracted to dry at the southern end. It is visited by flamingos at certain times of year, and there are bird hides to watch them. Look out for bushy clumps of the rare dwarf fan palm, Europe's only native palm.

Cathedral ★★

The Gothic cathedral stands on the site of the former mosque which was destroyed in the earthquake of 1522. Fortified to withstand pirate attack, it is a rather gaunt and ungainly building from outside, but inside it contains splendid choir stalls and a richly decorated altar in red and black jasper. ⓐ Plaza de la Catedral ⓣ 609 57 58 02 ⓞ Open Mon–Fri 10.00–16.30, Sat 10.00–13.00 ⓘ Admission charge

Cuevas de Sorbas (Caves of Sorbas) ★★

The extraordinary parched limestone scenery near Sorbas has created some weird formations, notably stalactite caves and deep gorges. ⓣ 950 36 47 04 ⓦ www.cuevasdesorbas.com ⓞ Different guided tours 10.00–20.00. Telephone to check ⓘ Admission charge

Mini Hollywood ★★

No local excursion programme fails to mention this attraction near Tabernas, north of Almería. There's a fair chance you've already seen it, for this film set and the surrounding desert-like scenery have featured in a number of classic 'spaghetti Westerns', notably the Sergio Leone films that made a big star out of Clint Eastwood, thanks to *A Fistful of Dollars*, *The Good, the Bad and the Ugly* and others. Visitors can wander round the slightly shabby 'town' and watch a cowboy show with plenty of shootings and horsing around. Next to Mini-Hollywood is a small zoo (separate entrance charge). ⓐ Carretera N340, Km 464 ⓣ 950 36 52 36 ⓞ Three shows daily: western, noon, 17.00 and 20.00; parrots, 11.00, 15.00 and 18.00; salon dancing, 13.00, 16.00 and 19.00 ⓘ Admission charge

EXCURSIONS

Museum of Almeria ★
Phoenician, Arab and ancient Greek objects discovered by Belgian engineer, Louis Siret. ⓐ Carretera de Ronda 2/6 ⓣ 950 26 44 92

Níjar ★★
The chief attraction of this pretty village is its handicrafts. The main street is lined with shops selling brightly coloured local pottery, esparto-grass baskets and cheerful stripy woven rag rugs or throws called *jarapas*.

Plaza Vieja ★
This charming, quiet square in the old town contains Almería's Ayuntamiento (town hall).

RESTAURANTS & BARS

Bodega Montenegro € Stacked with barrels, a very local traditional *tapas* bar near the cathedral. ⓐ Plaza Granero

Bodega del Patio € One of the city's best-loved bars. Typical old-fashioned decor. ⓐ Calle Real 84 ⓣ 950 23 09 07

Cafetería La Rambla €€ A smart boulevard café on one of the main streets. Good teas, cakes, and *platos combinados*. Tables outside. ⓐ Avenida Estación 2 ⓣ 950 27 19 63

Casa Puga €€ Tiles and marble deck the interior, and the tapas are excellent. ⓐ Calle Jovellanos 7 ⓣ 950 23 15 30 ⓒ Closed Sun and hols

La Gruta €€ A charming restaurant built into a grotto near the sea. Try the venison with truffles. ⓐ N340, Km 436 ⓣ 950 23 93 35

Restaurante Valentin €€ Smart seafood restaurant with a delicious and tempting menu, in the centre of town. ⓐ Calle Tenor Iribane 2 ⓣ 950 26 44 75 ⓦ www.restaurante-valentin.com

LIFESTYLE
Spanish life

LIFESTYLE

Food & drink

From the sophisticated restaurants of Marbella to the simple *chiringuito* beach bars of Torremolinos, or the hearty mountain cooking of the *pueblos blancos*, the cuisine of the Costa del Sol is as wide in variety as it is rich in flavours. For centuries Andalucía has been a land of different cultures, and their influences are reflected in the local food – the Phoenician style of salting, the Roman appreciation of olive oils and garlic, and the Arab taste for sweet dishes, exotic fruits and vegetables. The local cuisine is an ensemble of exotic, spicy dishes and bold, sun-drenched Mediterranean flavours, unique to southern Spain.

SOUPS

Popular starters include two chilled soups: *gazpacho andaluz* (made with tomato, garlic, sweet peppers and cucumber and served cold) and *ajo blanco* (made from garlic and almonds and served with grapes). Try also *sopa de pescado*, a tasty fish soup seasoned with tomato, onion, garlic and brandy, *guisado* made with fish and meat, and *potajes*, thick vegetable soups, which can frequently be found on menus in the mountains.

FRESH FISH

Fish is the main speciality of the coast. It's fun to lunch on fresh sardines, cooked over a wood fire by local fishermen on many of the beaches – they are cheap, tasty and usually served with fresh bread and salad. The daily catch in most resorts includes *bonito* (tuna), *pez espada* (swordfish), *rape* (monkfish), and *lenguado* (sole), all delicious grilled. Also worth a try are *pescaíto frito* (mixed fried fish), *gambas al pil-pil* (prawns sizzling in garlic and chilli), *calamares en su tinta* (squid cooked in its own ink), *risotto à la marinera* (seafood risotto) and, of course, *paella* – a scrumptious rice dish of meat, tomatoes, peppers, onions and a heap of seafood.

MEAT DISHES

Inland, a rich, traditional cuisine incorporates the game and wild herbs of the mountains, with hearty meat dishes including *estofado* (meat

◐ Lunch in the shade

stew), *fabada* (ham and bean stew), *conejo* (rabbit casserole) and *choto al ajo* (roast kid in garlic sauce). Look out also for *albondigas* (spicy meatballs), *calderetas* (lamb stew with almonds) and one of the most famous Andalucían dishes of all, *rabo de toro* (oxtail, prepared with tomatoes, onions and various spices). Food buffs should sample the many tasty local varieties of sausage and cured ham up in the hills.

VEGETARIANS

Vegetarians won't starve in Andalucía. Most menus include a choice of fresh salads, *tortilla* (omelette) and vegetable dishes, such as *garbanzos con espinacas* (chickpeas with spinach), *judías verdes con salsa de tomate* (green beans with tomato sauce) and *pisto de verduras* (ratatouille).

DESSERTS

Remember to save room for pudding – sweet, sticky *natillas* (cream custards), *yemas del tajo* (based on egg yolks and sugar), *brazo de gitano* (cream-filled pastries) and *piononos* (liqueur-soaked cakes) or some fresh fruit – oranges, peaches, grapes, raisins, pomegranates and figs – a typical way to round off a meal.

LIFESTYLE

An abundance of local produce can be found at markets

LIFESTYLE

BRITISH

If you're looking for a taste of home, most resorts can offer fish and chips, steak-and-kidney pie, ploughman's lunches and full English breakfasts, all washed down with a cuppa or a British beer.

INTERNATIONAL

There are few places in Spain with a greater concentration of restaurants to suit all tastes and budgets than the Costa del Sol. For something hot or spicy, there are Indian, Mexican, Chinese and Indonesian restaurants. If you prefer European, try the numerous French, Italian, German and Swiss restaurants. American fast-food outlets – McDonald's, Pizza Hut, KFC and Burger King – are all here as well.

TAPAS

This area of Spain is well known for tapas, small snacks served with drinks in most cafés and bars. The food is usually displayed on the bar so you can order it simply by pointing. The variety is endless – smoked ham, spicy sausage, cheese, olives, sardines, mushrooms, prawns, mussels, squid, octopus, anchovies, etc. They are served in small portions which allow you to sample several different dishes at once. Or you can follow the Andalucían custom of moving from bar to bar, sampling just one dish in each – a kind of Spanish-style pub-crawl!

DRINKS

Spanish wine is the perfect accompaniment for such a rich assortment of dishes, so be sure to try the sweet wines of Málaga. However, many Spaniards prefer beer, such as Cruzcampo and San Miguel.

Sherry is a popular tapas accompaniment. There are many different types to choose from, including *fino* (light, dry and pale yellow), *manzanilla* (dry and delicate), *oloroso* (sweet, dark and full-bodied) or *amontillado* (amber and medium-dry).

A favourite drink worth trying is *sangría* – a jug of red wine, rum or brandy, fruit and lemonade served chilled with ice. Or, for a special treat, try white *sangría*, made with sparkling white wine.

LIFESTYLE

Menu decoder

aceitunas aliñadas Marinated olives

albóndigas en salsa Meatballs in (usually tomato) sauce

albóndigas de pescado Fish cakes

allioli Garlic-flavoured mayonnaise served as an accompaniment to just about anything – a rice dish, vegetables, shellfish – or as a dip for bread

bistec or biftek Beef steak; rare is *poco hecho*, *regular* is medium and *muy hecho* is well done (ask for it more well cooked than at home)

bocadillo The Spanish sandwich, usually made of French-style bread

caldereta A stew based on fish or lamb

caldo A soup or broth

carne Meat; *carne de ternera* is beef; *carne picada* is minced meat; *carne de cerdo* is pork; *carne de cordero* is lamb

chorizo A cured, dry red-coloured sausage made from chopped pork, paprika, spices, herbs and garlic

churros Flour fritters cooked in spiral shapes in very hot fat and cut into strips, best dunked into hot chocolate

embutidos charcutería Pork meat preparations including *jamón* (ham), *chorizo* (see above), *salchichones* (sausages) and *morcillas* (black pudding)

ensalada Salad; the normal restaurant salad is composed of lettuce, onion, tomato and olives

ensalada mixta As above, but with extra ingredients, such as boiled egg, tuna fish or asparagus

escabeche A sauce of fish, meat or vegetables cooked in wine and vinegar and left to go cold

estofado de buey Beef stew, made with carrots and turnips, or with potatoes

fiambre Any type of cold meat such as ham, *chorizo*, etc

flan Caramel custard, the national dessert of Spain

fritura A fry up, as in *fritura de pescado* – different kinds of fried fish

gambas Prawns; *gambas a la plancha* are grilled, *gambas al ajillo* are fried with garlic and *gambas con gabardina* deep fried in batter

gazpacho andaluz Cold soup (originally from Andalucía) made from tomatoes, cucumbers, peppers, garlic and olive oil

gazpacho manchego (Not to be confused with *gazpacho andaluz*) a hot dish made with meat (chicken or rabbit) and unleavened bread

habas con jamón Broad beans fried with diced ham (sometimes with chopped hard boiled egg and parsley)

helado Ice cream

jamón Ham; *jamón serrano* and *jamón iberico* (far more expensive) are dry cured; cooked ham is *jamón de york*

langostinos a la plancha Large prawns grilled and served with vinaigrette or *allioli*; *langostinos a la marinera* are cooked in white wine

lenguado Sole, often served cooked with wine and mushrooms

mariscos shellfish

menestra A dish of mixed vegetables cooked separately and combined before serving

menú del día Set menu for the day at a fixed price; it may or may not include bread, wine and a dessert, but it doesn't usually include coffee

paella Famous rice dish originally from Valencia but now made all over Spain; *paella valenciana* has chicken and rabbit; *paella de mariscos* is made with seafood; *paella mixta* combines meat and seafood

pan Bread; *pan de molde* is sliced white bread; wholemeal is *pan integral*

pincho moruno Pork kebab: spicy chunks of pork on a skewer

pisto The Spanish version of ratatouille, made with tomato, peppers, onions, garlic, courgettes and aubergines

pollo al ajillo Chicken fried with garlic; *pollo a la cerveza* is cooked in beer; *pollo al chilindrón* is cooked with peppers, tomatoes and onions

salpicón de mariscos Seafood salad

sopa de ajo Delicious warming winter garlic soup thickened with bread, usually with a poached egg floating in it

tarta helada A popular ice cream cake served as dessert

cordero asado Roast lamb flavoured with lemon and white wine

tortilla de patatas The classic omelette, also called *tortilla española*, made with potatoes; it can be eaten hot or cold; if you want a plain omelette (with nothing in it) ask for a *tortilla francesa*

zarzuela de pescado y mariscos A stew made with white fish and shellfish in a tomato, wine and saffron stock

LIFESTYLE

Textiles shop, Costa de Almería

LIFESTYLE

Shopping

Shopping is one of the favourite pastimes for visitors to the Costa del Sol, with a huge range of things to buy and places to buy them.

MARKETS
Bargain hunters will love the hustle and bustle of the local markets. The best buys are fruit and vegetables, leather goods, ceramics and lace. Don't forget to barter, this is very normal at markets in Spain, so you won't be offending anyone – it's also great fun. Most major resorts along the coast have a morning market once a week. Fuengirola Market (Tues) has the reputation of being the biggest, cheapest and best, while the market in Nerja (Tues) is noted for its charm and atmosphere.

GIFTS & HANDICRAFTS
The best holiday buys here are local handicrafts, including lace, colourful ceramics, and attractive basketwork. You will find plenty of choice in the craft shops of Ronda, Mijas and other mountain villages. For shoes, handbags, belts and wallets, head to Córdoba, famous for its leather and also its filigree silverware. Granada is well known for its inlaid woodwork (such as music boxes and chess boards) while good buys in Sevilla include embroidered shawls and ceramics.

FASHIONS
Marbella and central Málaga are probably the best places for clothes shopping, with their chic boutiques and fashion stores. For trendy designer boutiques and a glamorous backdrop of millionaires' yachts, Puerto Banús is every shopper's paradise, even just for window-shopping. More affordable, and one of the best shopping streets on the coast is Torremolinos' Calle San Miguel, where you can find just about anything from leather goods to Lladró porcelain. The Costa del Sol is also a good place to buy sports clothing and equipment, especially at the end of the season. Mojácar is a good place to buy souvenirs and presents.

LIFESTYLE

Kids

There is plenty to amuse children on the Costa del Sol. Apart from the obvious pleasures of the beach or hotel pool, the area has masses of attractions aimed at entertaining youngsters of all ages. Many of the hotels organize children's programmes of fun, games and outings, and the tourist offices have lists of all the local attractions geared towards children.

ANIMAL MAGIC
There are a whole host of animal-orientated activities along the coast which are fun for children, including the Fuengirola Zoo, the Crocodile Park in Torremolinos and the spectacular shows of Andalucían horse dressage at El Ranchito, also near Torremolinos.

BOAT TRIPS
Older children will relish the idea of a boat excursion to explore the coastline. Most resorts offer trips, some include opportunities for swimming, diving and snorkelling too.

FAMILY RESTAURANTS
Spaniards adore children, which means they are welcome almost everywhere, notably in restaurants (even late at night). Some have high chairs available and most have children's choices on the menu. If not, just ask, and the restaurant is more than likely to offer child-size portions.

MINI-TRAINS
Most resorts have a mini-train, enabling mum and dad to see the sights while keeping the kids happy at the same time.

SPORTS
When the family has tired of the beach, why not have a quick round of mini-golf, take them horse riding or, for an exciting afternoon, try a few circuits of go-karting.

🔺 *Mini-train: see the sights and keep the kids happy*

TIVOLI WORLD

There are lots of thrills and great entertainment to be had in the Tivoli wonderland, the largest amusement park on the Costa. Kids can have a go on all their favourite fairground rides like the waltzers, the big wheel, the ghost train and the dodgems, as well as seeing some traditional flamenco, Western or circus shows – a great day out for children young and old.

WATER FUN PARKS

A splashing time is guaranteed for all the family at the Aquapark, Torremolinos and the Parque Aquático, Mijas, with a variety of activities including the largest water-slide in Europe, wave machines, pools, rapids and even a mini aquatic park for small children.

LIFESTYLE

Sports & activities

CYCLING
Cycling and mountain biking are excellent ways to enjoy the Andalucían countryside. The tourist board has a guide covering 120 itineraries, with maps, hill profiles, time required and difficulty ratings available from most tourist information offices. Two reliable bike-hire shops are:
Xtrem Bike ⓐ Las Mercedes 14, Torremolinos ⓣ 952 38 06 91; and
Motomercado (ⓐ Calle Santa Rosa 18, Los Boliches ⓣ 952 47 25 51 ⓦ www.rentabike.org

GOLF
The Costa del Sol is often called the Costa del Golf and not without reason. With 40-plus courses within just 120 km (75 miles) of coastline, it is Europe's number-one winter golf destination, with some of the finest courses in the world. Most courses demand a handicap certificate and in high season (Jan–May, Sept–Nov), book tee-times well in advance.
Valderrama Setting of the 1997 Ryder Cup. ⓐ Carretera N340, Km 132 ⓣ 956 79 57 50/79 12 00
Los Arqueros Golf Founded by world-champion Manuel Pinero – tuition at all levels. ⓐ Carretera de Ronda, Km 42.9 ⓣ 952 78 46 00
Sotogrande ⓐ Carretera N340, Km 132 ⓣ 956 79 50 50
Mijas Golf ⓐ Carretera Coín, Km 3 ⓣ 952 47 68 43
Marbella Golf and Country Club ⓐ Carretera N340, Km 187 ⓣ 952 83 05 00
La Dama de Noche A 9-hole course, offers floodlit golf, enabling tee off as late as 22.00 ⓐ Camino del Angel, Marbella ⓣ 952 81 81 50

HORSE RIDING
San Pedro Riding School, near town, organizes treks in the countryside.
ⓐ Carril del Potril, San Pedro ⓣ 952 78 81 89
Club Hípico at Alhauín Golf – a traditional Andalucían-style farmhouse with restaurant, bar and tennis as well as riding. ⓐ Carretera Fuengirola-Alhaurín El Grande ⓣ 952 59 58 00

JEEP SAFARIS

Discover rural Spain by jeep with **Niza Cars** of Torremolinos ❶ 952 38 14 48 or **Marbella Rangers** ❶ 952 83 30 82

SCUBA DIVING

Nerja's crystal-clear water is a good place for beginners. Useful contacts include: **Club de Buceo** ❶ 952 56 23 65 in Benalmádena; **Aquatech** ❶ 952 66 03 27 in Fuengirola; and **Club Náutique** ❶ 952 52 46 54 in Nerja

SKIING

North-east of Nerja, the Sierra Nevada is the most southerly ski region in Europe and one of the highest. Its most popular ski resort, is just 31 km (19 miles) from Granada. **Solynieve** ❶ 958 24 91 00 Ⓦ http://spain.skireport.com for ski reports

TENNIS

Many resort hotels have tennis courts, and many clubs organize regular summer tournaments and other programmes. Among the smartest are: **Manolo Santana Racket Club** ⓐ Urbanizacion Puente Romano; and **Club de Tenis Lew Hoad** ⓐ Urbanizacion Campo de Tenis ❶ 952 47 48 58

WATERSKIING

Water-skiing is available from most marinas and also at **Funny Beach**, the water sports centre just east of Marbella ⓐ Carretera N340, Km 184 ❶ 952 82 33 59 Ⓦ www.funnybeach.net. Alternatively, **Cable Ski Marbella**, offers the perfect way for beginners to learn – in calm waters and without a boat! Instead an overhead cable takes you round an 800 m (0.5 mile) circuit ❶ 952 78 55 79 Ⓦ www.marbellacableski.com

WINDSURFING & KITESURFING

The main windsurfing/kitesurfing season runs from March to November here. Just beyond Gibraltar, Tarifa is the windsurfing capital of Europe, just 14 km (9 miles) from the coast of North Africa.

Festivals & events

FLAMENCO

Flamenco originates from Andalucía, with Moorish origins that can be heard in the dance's wailing chants. There are two types of flamenco – the slow, emotional *Cante Jondo* (deep song) and the bright, cheerful *Cante Chico* (light song), with rousing melodies and, of course, the wonderful, rhythmic clapping, stamping and castanet playing. With the men in their slim, Córdoban suits and the women in sweeping, ruffled gypsy dresses, the dance offers excitement and colour second to none:

Los Gallos ⓐ Plaza de Santa Cruz, Sevilla ⓣ 954 21 69 81 ⓛ Nightly at 21.00 and 23.30

Ali Oli ⓐ Paseo Marítimo, Fuengirola ⓛ Fri nights

Pepe Lopez ⓐ Plaza de la Gamba Alegre, Torremolinos ⓣ 952 38 12 84 ⓛ Mon–Sat nights

▲ *Traditional Spanish fans*

Tablao Cardenal Calle Torrijos, Córdoba 10   957 48 31 12
 Wed–Sun at 22.30
Sala Flamenco Don de Maña Estadío Municipal, Marbella   Mon–Sat at 23.00

FESTIVALS

Every town has a *feria* (festival) to celebrate their patron saint's day and these festivals usually involve lively parades, music, dancing, food, wine, street processions and sometimes bull-fights, funfairs and circuses. At night, vast paellas are cooked over an open fire and the celebrations continue with singing, flamenco and fireworks. The largest and most spectacular is in Málaga in August. For more details consult
 www.andalucia.com/festival

LIFESTYLE

Colourful boats adorn the beaches

VIRGEN DEL CARMEN

If you happen to take a holiday on the Costa del Sol on 16 July, you should make an effort to catch this colourful and lively fiesta. Essentially, it's a 'blessing of the waters' ceremony, a reminder that those big holiday resorts were once just simple fishing communities. There are several days of events which culminate in a splendid procession in which the patron saint of fishermen is carried from the church into the sea. The celebrations take place in several places, but are especially magnificent in **Los Boliches, Fuengirola**.

PRACTICAL INFORMATION
Tips and advice

PRACTICAL INFORMATION

Preparing to go

GETTING THERE
The cheapest way to get to the Costa del Sol or the Costa de Almería is to book a package holiday. If your travelling times are flexible, and you can avoid the school holidays, look for cheap last-minute deals on websites or in such papers as the *Sunday Telegraph*, and *The Sunday Times*.

BY AIR
The main airport for the Costa del Sol is at Málaga, but some airlines also fly to Sevilla and Jerez. The Costa de Almería is accessible from Málaga and from the airport at Almería.

BEFORE YOU LEAVE
It is not necessary to have inoculations to travel in Europe, but make sure you and your family are up to date with the basics, such as tetanus. It is a good idea to pack a well-stocked first-aid kit. Sun lotion can be more expensive than in the UK so it is worth taking a good selection. Take enough of your prescription medicines with you – they may be difficult to obtain in Spain. It is also worth having a dental check-up.

DOCUMENTS
The most important documents you will need are your tickets and your passport. Check well in advance that your passport is up to date and has at least three months left to run (six months is even better). All children, including newborn babies, need their own passport now, unless they are already included on the passport of the person they are travelling with. It generally takes at least three weeks to process a passport renewal. For the latest information, contact the **Passport Agency** ❶ 0870 521 0410 ⓦ www.ukpa.gov.uk Check the details of your travel tickets well before your departure, ensuring that the timings and dates are correct.

If you are thinking of hiring a car while you are away, you will need to have your UK driving licence with you. If you want more than one driver for the car, the other drivers must have their licence too.

PRACTICAL INFORMATION

MONEY

You will need some currency before you go, especially if your flight gets you to your destination at the weekend or late in the day after the banks have closed.

Traveller's cheques are the safest way to carry money because the money will be refunded if the cheques are lost or stolen. To buy traveller's cheques or exchange money at a bank you may need to give up to a week's notice, depending on the quantity of foreign currency you require. You can exchange money at the airport before you depart. You should also make sure that your credit, charge and debit cards are up to date – you do not want them to expire mid holiday – and that your credit limit is sufficient to allow you to make those holiday purchases.

Don't forget, too, to check your PIN numbers in case you haven't used them for a while – you may want to draw money from cash dispensers while you are away. Ring your bank or card company and they will help you out.

INSURANCE

Have you got sufficient cover for your holiday? Check that your policy covers you adequately for loss of possessions and valuables, for activities you might want to try – such as scuba-diving, horse riding, or water-sports – and for emergency medical and dental treatment, including flights home if required.

After January 2006, a new EHIC card replaces the E111 form to allow UK visitors access to reduced-cost, and sometimes free state-provided medical treatment in the EEA. For further information, ring EHIC enquiries line: 0845 605 0707 or visit the Department of Health website www.dh.gov.uk

> ### TELEPHONING COSTA DEL SOL
> To call Costa del Sol from the UK, dial 00 34 then the nine-digit number – there's no need to wait for a dialling tone.

PRACTICAL INFORMATION

SECURITY

Take sensible precautions to prevent your house being burgled while you are away:

- Cancel milk, newspapers and other regular deliveries so that post and milk does not pile up on the doorstep, indicating that you are away.
- Let the postman know where to leave parcels and bulky mail that will not go through your letterbox – ideally with a next-door neighbour.
- If possible, arrange for a friend or neighbour to visit regularly, closing and opening curtains in the evening and morning, and switching lights on and off to give the impression that the house is being lived in.
- Consider buying electrical timing devices that will switch lights and radios on and off, again to give the impression that there is someone in the house.
- Let Neighbourhood Watch representatives know that you will be away so that they can keep an eye on your home.
- If you have a burglar alarm, make sure that it is serviced and working properly and is switched on when you leave (you may find that your insurance policy requires this). Ensure that a neighbour is able to gain access to the alarm to turn it off if it is set off accidentally.
- If you are leaving cars unattended, put them in a garage, if possible, and leave a key with a neighbour in case the alarm goes off.

AIRPORT PARKING AND ACCOMMODATION

If you intend to leave your car in an airport car park while you are away, or stay the night at an airport hotel before or after your flight, you should book well ahead to take advantage of discounts or cheap off-airport parking. Check whether the hotel offers free parking for the duration of the holiday – often the savings made on parking costs can significantly reduce the accommodation price.

PACKING TIPS

Baggage allowances vary according to the airline, destination and the class of travel, but 20kg (44lb) per person is the norm for luggage that is carried in the hold (it usually tells you what the weight limit is on your

PRACTICAL INFORMATION

ticket). You are also allowed one item of cabin baggage weighing no more than 5kg (11lb), and measuring 46 by 30 by 23cm (18 by 12 by 9 inches). In addition, you can usually carry your duty-free purchases, umbrella, handbag, coat, camera, etc, as hand baggage. Large items – surfboards, golf-clubs, collapsible wheelchairs and pushchairs – are usually charged as extras and it is a good idea to let the airline know in advance that you want to bring these.

CHECK-IN, PASSPORT CONTROL AND CUSTOMS

First-time travellers can often find airport security intimidating, but it is all very easy, really.

- Check-in desks usually open two or three hours before the flight is due to depart. Arrive early for the best choice of seats.
- Look for your flight number on the monitors in the check-in area, and find the relevant check-in desk. Your tickets will be checked and your luggage taken. Take your boarding card and go to the departure gate. Here your hand luggage will be X-rayed and your passport checked.
- In the departure area, you can shop and relax, but watch the monitors that tell you when to board – usually about 30 minutes before take-off. Go to the departure gate shown on the monitor and follow the instructions given to you by the airline staff.

CURRENCY

Currency Euro (a) note denominations are 500, 200, 100, 50, 20, 10 and 5. Coins are 1 and 2 euros and 1, 2, 5, 10, 20 and 50 céntimos. A euro equals 166.386 pesetas.

Banks In winter most banks are open 0830–1400 Monday to Friday and until noon on Saturday although these hours may vary slightly from branch to branch. Summer hours are shorter, usually 0830 until 1330 or 1400.

Exchange bureaux Look out for the sign 'Cambio'; these are generally open seven days a week 1000–2100 but hours vary widely.

Credit Cards All major credit cards are accepted, but cash is preferred in more rural areas. Holders of Visa and MasterCard can use the 24-hour automatic cash dispensers, which have instructions in English.

PRACTICAL INFORMATION

During your stay

BEACHES
In summer, many beaches have lifeguards and a flag safety system. Other beaches may be safe for swimming but there are unlikely to be lifeguards or life-saving amenities available. Bear in mind that the strong winds that develop in the hotter months can quickly change a safe beach into a not-so-safe one, and some can have strong currents the further out that you go. If in doubt, ask your local representative or at your hotel.

> **BEACHES**
> Look out for the flag safety system:
> - **Green** = safe bathing and swimming
> - **Yellow** = strong swimmers only
> - **Red** = no swimming

CONSULATES
The British Consulate is at Plaza Nueva 87, 41001 Seville 954 22 88 74 and Calle Mauricio Moro Pareto, 2 Málaga 952 35 23 00.

ELECTRICITY
The current in Spain is 220v-AC with two-pin, round-pronged plugs. Adaptors can be found in many hypermarkets, supermarkets and also some electrical stores. If you can, take one with you to be on the safe side. Most hotels and pensiones have electric points for hair dryers and shavers in all the bedrooms. If you are considering buying electrical appliances to take home, always check that they will work in your country before you buy.

FACILITIES FOR VISITORS WITH DISABILITIES
Modern buildings generally have adequate provision for the disabled, with lifts, ramps and special toilet facilities. However, owing to their

PRACTICAL INFORMATION

construction, entry to certain historical monuments may be restricted. Local tourist offices, or the monument staff, can provide information about wheelchair access.

GETTING AROUND

Car hire and driving As well as international car hire companies, a few Spanish companies, such as Atesa, operate nationwide. You can probably negotiate the best deal with an international company from home. There are also fly-drive and other package deals, including car hire. Fly-drive, an option for two or more travellers, can be arranged by travel agents. There are car hire desks at airports and offices in the large towns. Alternatively, if you wish to hire a car locally for, say, a week or less, you can arrange it with a local travel agent. A car for hire is called a *coche de alquiler*. Car-hire prices and conditions vary according to the region and locality.

Visitors driving vehicles from other countries need no special documentation in Spain, but make sure you have all the relevant papers from your country of origin, your driving licence, vehicle registration document and insurance. Your insurance company should be able to arrange an overseas extension of your car insurance. To hire a car in Spain you need show only a current driving licence. When driving from Britain, if you have an old-style green licence you will need to purchase an International Driving Permit., obtained from the RAC or the AA.

Most Spanish motorways are well equipped with an SOS network of telephones, which provide instant access to the emergency services. Ask for *auxilio en carretera*. In Spain people drive on the right, so you must give way to the right. At roundabouts, you should give way to cars already on the roundabout but be extremely careful when on a roundabout yourself: do not expect oncoming cars to stop. Some will disregard you and drive straight on.

The speed limits are 50 km/h (30 mph) in built-up areas; 90–100 km/h (55–60 mph) outside them and 120 km/h (75 mph) on motorways. Seat belts are compulsory in the back and front; motor cyclists must wear crash helmets. Drivers must carry two warning triangles and can be fined by the traffic police for not being equipped with a first-aid kit.

PRACTICAL INFORMATION

Taxis These are essential for access to out-of-town nightspots. You can phone from your hotel reception area, walk to a taxi rank, or flag one down as it passes by. A green light in the front window or on top of the roof indicates that the taxi is available for hire. Taxis are always white and have a logo on the doors, which displays their official number. Drivers rarely speak any English, so learn enough Spanish to explain where you are going and to negotiate the fare. The meter marks up the basic fare; however, supplements maybe added for *tarifa nocturna* (night driving), *maletas* (luggage), or *dias festivos* (public holidays). If in doubt of the correct price, ask for the *tarifas* (price list).

PUBLIC TRANSPORT

Buses Various private bus companies provide regular links between major resorts and outlying villages. Buses run frequently (every 20–30 minutes) within and between resorts and are reasonably priced. Board buses at the front, and get off at the rear of the bus. You usually buy your ticket from the driver or you can buy strips of ten tickets called *bonobus* from *estancos* (tobacconists) and stationers. It is not unusual for buses to be crowded.

Trains An excellent train service, with air-conditioning and announcements in Spanish and English, runs between Málaga and Fuengirola, stopping at the airport, Torremolinos and Arroyo de la Miel. Trains operate every 30 minutes at the airport, in either direction, daily from 06.45 to 23.00. The full journey takes 42 minutes.

Mountain bikes, scooters and motorbikes These can be hired from various outlets. Crash helmets are obligatory. Details of hire can be obtained from tourist offices.

HEALTH MATTERS

Pharmacies *Farmácias* are easily recognized by a large green or red cross. Their staff will be able to suggest remedies for minor medical problems. They are open 09.30–13.30, 17.00–20.30 Monday to Friday. After these times and on Saturdays and Sundays, there will always be a 'duty' chemist open, details of which will be posted on every chemist's window.

PRACTICAL INFORMATION

If in need of urgent medical assistance, go to the nearest *Urgencias*, the emergency ward of a hospital or clinic. All the cities have several hospitals each, while the Costa del Sol has a hospital situated on the main coastal highway (N340) just east of Marbella (Hospital Costa del Sol, Carretera Nacional N340, Km 187, Marbella, Málaga). Most hospitals have volunteer interpreters who speak English and occasionally also other languages.

If you need to use your E111 form (or EHIC Card, see page 113), do not part with the original, but hand over a photocopy instead.

If you have private travel insurance, make sure you have your policy on you when requesting medical assistance. Depending on the insurance company, you may be expected to pay treatment and be reimbursed at a later date.

Beware of the sun, particularly from May to October when temperatures can reach up to 45°C (113°F). Try to avoid walking in the midday sun and stay in the shade whenever possible. Drink plenty of bottled mineral water. It is advisable to wear sunglasses and a hat when you are out sightseeing.

THE LANGUAGE

The Spanish respond warmly to visitors who attempt to speak a little of their language. Here are a few words and phrases to get you going:

ENGLISH	SPANISH (pronunciation)
General vocabulary	
yes	*sí* (see)
no	*no* (no)
please	*por favor* (por faBOR)
thank you (very much)	*(muchas) gracias* (MOOchas GRAtheeyas)
You're welcome	*de nada* (deNAda)
hello	*hola* (Ola)
goodbye	*adiós* (adeeYOS)
good morning/day	*buenos días* (BWEnos DEEyas)
good afternoon/evening	*buenas tardes* (BWEnas TARdes)

PRACTICAL INFORMATION

ENGLISH	SPANISH (pronunciation)

General vocabulary

good evening (after dark)/night	*buenas noches* (BWEnas NOches)
excuse me (to get attention or to get past)	*¡disculpe!* (desKOOLpay)
excuse me (to apologize or to ask pardon)	*¡perdón!* (perDON)
Sorry	*lo siento* (lo seeYENtoe)
Help!	*¡socorro!* (SOHcohroe)
today	*hoy* (oy)
tomorrow	*mañana* (manYAna)
yesterday	*ayer* (ayYER)

Useful words and phrases

open	*abierto* (abeeYERtoe)
closed	*cerrado* (therRAdoe)
push	*empujar* (empooYAR)
pull	*tirar* (teeRAR)
How much is it?	*¿Cuánto es?* (KWANtoe es)
bank	*el banco* (el BANko)
bureau de change	*la oficina de cambio* (la ofeeTHEEna de KAMbeeyo)
post office	*correos* (koRAYos)
duty (all-night) chemist	*la farmacia de guardia* (la farMAHtheeya de garDEEya)
bank card	*la tarjeta de banco* (la tarHEHta de BANko)
credit card	*la tarjeta de crédito* (la tarHEHta de CREdeetoe)
traveller's cheques	*los cheques de viaje* (los CHEkes de beeAhay)
table	*la mesa* (la MEHsa)
menu	*el menú/la carta* (el menOO/la KARta)
waiter	*el/la camarero/a* (el/la kahmahRERo/a)

PRACTICAL INFORMATION

ENGLISH
Useful words and phrases

ENGLISH	SPANISH (pronunciation)
water	*agua* (Agwa)
fizzy/still water	*agua con/sin gas* (Agwa con/sin gas)
I don't understand	*no entiendo* (No enteeYENdoe)
The bill, please	*La cuenta, por favor* (la KWENta, por faBOR)
Do you speak English?	*¿Habla usted inglés?* (Ablah OOsted eenGLES)
My name is...	*Me llamo ...* (meh YAmoh ...)
Where are the toilets?	*¿Dónde están los servicios?* (DONdeh esTAN los serBEEtheeos)
Can you help me?	*¿Puede ayudarme?* (PWEday ayooDARmeh)

OPENING HOURS

Shops Spanish shops tend to close during the afternoon siesta (except for department stores and touristy souvenir shops in the large towns). Most shops open at 09.30 and close at 13.30. They usually reopen about 17.00 or 17.30 and stay open until 20.30 or 21.00. These times will obviously vary from shop to shop.

Museums Hours kept by monuments and museums vary considerably, so it is best to check before you visit. Most close on Sunday afternoons. However, during the tourist season many museums stay open all day.

Churches Most churches open only for Mass, but in small towns a caretaker will often let visitors in between religious services. Mass is held every hour on Sundays, and at about 19.00 – 21.00 on weekdays. In most churches, tourists are welcome in the church during a service as long as they are quiet. Dress codes are not as strict as in other Catholic countries but avoid skimpy shorts and bare arms. There is usually no admission charge, although a donation may be expected.

Banks In Andalucía banks are open for business from 08.30 to 14.00 Monday to Friday but only from 08.30 to 13.00 on Saturdays during the winter. From May to September they do not open on Saturdays. Banks

PRACTICAL INFORMATION

are never open on public holidays and during a town's annual feria week the banks will open for just three hours from 09.00 hours to noon, to allow staff to join in the merrymaking.

PERSONAL COMFORT AND SECURITY

Pickpockets are common in crowded areas, especially outside monuments and at markets. Be particularly wary of people asking you the time, as they are probably trying to distract you while someone else attempts to snatch your bag or wallet. Use traveller's cheques, Eurocheques or credit cards rather than cash and carry a photocopy of your passport, leaving the original in the hotel safe. If you have a car, do not leave valuables in view and try to leave it in a security-controlled car park. In the event of being robbed or attacked, try to report the incident to the police (*poner una denuncia*) as soon as possible (at least within 24 hours). This is extremely important if you wish to obtain a statement (*denuncia*) to make an insurance claim.

The abundance of street-life means that you will rarely find yourself alone or in a position to be harassed. However, women may be intimidated by men passing comment as they walk by, or even following them. This pastime, known as *piropo*, is common and not meant as a serious threat. Do not use maps late at night, and try to look like you know where you are going. Make sure that you take official taxis displaying a licence number and avoid public transport at night if alone. Any cab driver touting for business is likely to be illegal.

When in the countryside, you may see signs showing a bull or saying *Toro bravo* (fighting bull). Take these signs seriously – bulls are extremely dangerous and by no means should be approached.

There are three types of police in Spain, the Guardia Civil, the Policía Nacional and the Policía Local. When approaching the police remember that it is illegal to be without ID. The Policía Nacional, who wear a blue uniform, are the best to turn to, especially when reporting a crime. They have many different responsibilities, including dealing with visitors' permits and documentation.The Policía Local take care of the day-to-day policing of small towns and villages.

PRACTICAL INFORMATION

> **EMERGENCY TELEPHONE NUMBERS**
> **First Aid** 061   **Police** 091   **Traffic police:**
> Sevilla 954 62 11 11
> Córdoba 957 20 30 33
> Granada 958 15 36 00
>
> **PHONING ABROAD**
> To call an overseas number from the UK, dial **oo** (the international access code), then the country code (**44**), then the area code (minus the initial **0**), then the number.

If you are not happy with a service, particularly in a restaurant or hotel, you are entitled to ask for the *Libro de Reclamaciones*. This is an official complaints book at the disposal of customers, which is inspected periodically by the local authorities. Only use it for very unsatisfactory affairs or just threaten to use it if you suspect you are being cheated.
Public toilets These are scarce. However, there is a bar on virtually every corner which is legally bound to allow you to use their toilets. Nevertheless some bars do so reluctantly, if no purchase has been made. A 'D' on the door stands for *Damas* (ladies), and a 'C' indicates *Caballeros* (men). Keep small change handy because if the toilets are not coin-operated, it is usual to leave some small change for the attendant.

POST OFFICES

The Spanish postal service is rightly known as slow and unreliable. Postcards sent abroad can take more than a month to arrive. Letters posted at a central post office will usually arrive in reasonable time, but be aware that post-boxes (*buzones*) may not be emptied for days. If you need to send important or urgent mail use the *certificado* (registered) and *urgente* (express) mail. Buy stamps (*sellos*) at post offices and *estancos* (tobacconists), displaying a distinctive yellow and red sign. Main post offices are open 08.30–20.30 Mon–Fri, 09.30–14.00 Sat.

PRACTICAL INFORMATION

TELEPHONES

There are plenty of phone booths (*cabinas telefónicas*) on the streets, and most bars have public phones. There are also public telephone offices (*locutorios*), where you make a call and pay for it afterwards, and also private bureaux with phone and fax facilities. Public phones use coins and phonecards (*tarjetas telefónicas*). Cabinas are often positioned in pairs on streets, one accepting coins and one phonecards. You can buy phonecards from all tobacconists (*estancos*) and news stands. They are priced according to their value in call units. It is easiest to make long distance calls (*conferencias interurbanas*) at *locutorios*. A call made from a *cabina telefónica* or *locutorio* costs 35 per cent more than from a private phone.

Most of the new public phones booths have a visual display to guide users. Illustrated instructions, and lists of local and national dialling codes, are posted up in most booths in cities and centres of tourism.

TIME DIFFERENCES

Spain is one hour ahead of Greenwich Mean Time (GMT) and British Summer Time. The 24-hour clock is used in listings and for official purposes, but not in speech.

TIPPING

Tipping tends to be an issue of discretion in Spain. A service charge (*servicio*) is usually included in bills, but it is common to tip up to 10 per cent in addition and to give small change to petrol pump attendants, taxi drivers, and porters.

TOURIST OFFICES

Contact the Spanish National Tourist Office, 22–23 Manchester Square, London W1M 5AP ☎ 020 7486 8077 ☎ 020 7486 8034. It is best to write or visit in person, or you can consult the Spanish National Tourist Office website at ⓦ www.tourspain.es

INDEX

INDEX

A
Aguadulce 54
airports 112, 114, 115
Alhambra Palace 10, 84, 86
Almería 9, 92-4
Almerimar 50-1
Almuñecar 46
Andalucía 9
Antequera 80
aquariums 20, 37, 38
archaeological sites 16, 46, 71, 80, 81
art galleries 26, 37, 58, 78, 82

B
Balcón de Europa 46
banks 121
baths 16, 66
beaches, *see individual locations*
Benalmádena Costa 8, 36-41, 107
boat trips 10, 27, 31, 37, 51, 56, 88, 104
bonsai 26
bowling 17
bullrings 10, 66, 68
bus tours 56

C
cable cars 38, 63
cable-skiing 17
Cabo de Gata 92-3
car hire 117
casinos 22, 41
castles and fortresses 9, 13, 47, 59, 64, 70, 71, 80, 81, 92
cathedrals 10, 58, 72, 81, 86, 93
cave paintings 9, 46, 71, 91
caves 9, 46, 64, 71, 81, 84, 93
children 10, 13, 31, 36, 38, 104-5
churches and chapels 16, 47, 66, 71, 74, 80, 86, 110, 121
Competa 81
Córdoba 9, 72, 76-9, 103
Costa Natura 13
credit cards 115
Crocodile Park 43, 104
currency 113, 115
cycling 9, 27, 38, 53, 106, 118

D
dolphin watching 10, 31, 37, 63, 88
donkey-taxis 10, 72
driving 117

E
emergency telephone numbers 123
Estepona 12-15
excursions 27, 55-94

F
facilities for visitors with disabilities 116-17
festivals and events 36, 108-10
fishing 88
flamenco 10, 29, 39, 49, 56, 61, 69, 77, 79, 84, 108, 109
food and drink 10, 96-101
Frigiliana 10, 47, 70
Fuengirola 8, 10, 30-5, 72, 103, 104

G
gardens 10, 58, 59, 80, 82, 84, 86
Generalife gardens 10, 84, 86
Gibraltar 8, 10, 62-5
golf 13, 14, 16, 20, 25, 37, 51, 74, 106
gorges 66, 68, 71, 81
Granada 9, 10, 84-7, 103

H
health matters 118-19
horse and carriage tours 46, 72
horse dressage 43, 104
horse riding 18, 38, 106

I
the indalo 91
insurance 113, 122
Isla Mágica 58

INDEX

K
karting 26, 31, 104
kitesurfing 27, 107

L
La Mezquita 9, 77
La Puebla del Vicar 54
language 100-1, 119-21
Las Alpujarras 9

M
Málaga 10, 72, 80-3, 99, 103, 109
Marbella 8, 10, 24-9, 103, 106
marinas 10, 13, 26, 36, 38, 44, 51, 107
markets 10, 15, 18, 23, 32, 36, 47, 54, 78, 103
Maro 47
menu decoder 100-1
Mijas 10, 70, 72-5, 103, 105
Mini Hollywood 93
Mojácar 8, 10, 70, 88-91, 92, 103
museums 26, 38, 58, 59, 63, 68, 74, 78, 86, 94, 121

N
nature parks and reserves 27, 52, 63, 82
Nerja 10, 46-9, 103, 107
Nijar 94
nudist beaches 13

O
Ojén 27
opening hours 65, 121

P
palaces 10, 20, 66, 68, 71, 78, 84, 86
photography 66, 74, 84
Picasso Museums 82
post offices 123
pueblos blancos 9, 10, 36, 66, 70-1, 72, 88-9, 96
Puerto Banús 10, 20-3, 103

R
rock-climbing 81
Ronda 10, 66-9, 103
Roquetas 52-3
Roquetas de Mar 52

S
safari park 14
sailing 26, 53
Salobreña 47
San Pedro de Alcántara 16-19, 106
scooters 38, 118
scuba diving 18, 26, 107
Sevilla 9, 10, 56-61, 103
shopping 103, *see also individual locations*
skiing 107
Sotogrande 14

T
Tarifa 107
tennis 74, 107
theatre 36
Tivoli World 36, 39, 105
Torremolinos 8, 10, 42-5, 103, 104, 105
towers 59, 64, 77

V
vegetarians 97
Virgen del Carmen 110

W
walking 9, 66, 81
water parks 31, 43, 52, 89, 105
water sports 18, 26, 36, 44, 51, 88, 104
waterskiing 17, 18, 27, 107
white towns, *see pueblos blancos*
wildlife 27, 52, 63, 71, 93
windsurfing 26, 27, 53, 107
wine 10, 47, 81, 99

Z
zoos 31, 93, 104

ACKNOWLEDGEMENTS

ACKNOWLEDGEMENTS

We would like to thank all the photographers, picture libraries and organizations for the loan of the photographs reproduced in this book, to whom copyright in the photograph belongs:
Turismo Andaluz (pages 89, 102);
Teresa Fisher (pages 33, 98);
Lindsay Hunt (pages 13, 19);
Jupiter Images Corporation (pages 111, 125);
Pictures Colour Library (pages 8, 70, 79);
Eric Roberts (page 50);
Thomas Cook Tour Operations Ltd (pages 1, 5, 11, 35, 37, 42, 55, 61, 64, 67, 73, 83, 97, 105, 108, 110).

We would also like to thank the following for their contribution to this series:
John Woodcock (map and symbols artwork);
Becky Alexander, Patricia Baker, Sophie Bevan, Judith Chamberlain-Webber, Nicky Gyopari, Stephanie Horner, Krystyna Mayer, Robin Pridy (editorial support);
Christine Engert, Suzie Johanson, Richard Lloyd, Richard Peters, Alistair Plumb, Jane Prior, Barbara Theisen, Ginny Zeal, Barbara Zuñiga (Design support).

Send your thoughts to
books@thomascook.com

- Found a beach bar, peaceful stretch of sand or must-see sight that we don't feature?
- Like to tip us off about any information that needs a little updating?
- Want to tell us what you love about this handy, little guidebook and more importantly how we can make it even handier?

Then here's your chance to tell all! Send us ideas, discoveries and recommendations today and then look out for your valuable input in the next edition of this title. And, as an extra 'thank you' from Thomas Cook Publishing, you'll be automatically entered into our exciting monthly prize draw.

Email to the above address or write to:
HotSpots Project Editor, Thomas Cook Publishing, PO Box 227, Unit 15/16, Coningsby Road, Peterborough PE3 8SB, UK.